Lexical meaning as a testable hypothesis

## Studies in Functional and Structural Linguistics (SFSL)

ISSN 1385-7916

Taking the broadest and most general definitions of the terms functional and structural, this series aims to present linguistic and interdisciplinary research that relates language structure – at any level of analysis from phonology to discourse – to broader functional considerations, whether cognitive, communicative, pragmatic or sociocultural. Preference will be given to studies that focus on data from actual discourse, whether speech, writing or other nonvocal medium.

The series was formerly known as *Linguistic & Literary Studies in Eastern Europe (LLSEE)*.

For an overview of all books published in this series, please see
*http://benjamins.com/catalog/sfsl*

### Volume 75

Lexical meaning as a testable hypothesis
The case of English *look, see, seem* and *appear*
by Nadav Sabar

# Lexical meaning
# as a testable hypothesis

The case of English *look*, *see*, *seem* and *appear*

Nadav Sabar

John Benjamins Publishing Company

Amsterdam / Philadelphia

The paper used in this publication meets the minimum requirements of the American National Standard for Information Sciences – Permanence of Paper for Printed Library Materials, ANSI z39.48-1984.

DOI 10.1075/sfsl.75

Cataloging-in-Publication Data available from Library of Congress:
LCCN 2017056558 (PRINT) / 2018000707 (E-BOOK)

ISBN 978 90 272 0042 6 (HB)
ISBN 978 90 272 6434 3 (E-BOOK)

John Benjamins Publishing Company · https://benjamins.com

# Table of contents

# Acknowledgements

I am grateful to the Columbia University Seminar on Columbia School Linguistics for the many occasions it afforded me to present data and analysis pertaining to this study. I am also grateful for the Columbia School Linguistics Society Graduate Student Fellowship which has been awarded to me for the 2014–15 academic year, during which time most of this manuscript was written. I would like to thank all attendants of the Columbia School Seminar for their contribution to my development of this project; particularly Wallis Reid, Ricardo Otheguy, Alan Huffman, Joseph Davis, Nancy Stern and Radmila Gorup. Our discussions at seminar have always been intellectually stimulating and nurturing, and most invaluable in the development of the hypotheses presented in this manuscript. Of course, acknowledgement in no way implies that the above individuals agree with everything written here; all errors are mine.

I would like to specially thank Wallis Reid, with whom I have engaged in hundreds of email correspondences, ranging from the littlest to the most substantial of questions. Beginning from my first introduction to Columbia School linguistics in 2011, I have insistently raised many challenges to this theoretical framework, and Wallis has consistently taken the time to engage with me, thoroughly educating me in CS linguistics and providing me with the tools necessary to do this research.

Ricardo Otheguy has been the most rigorous reader of my work, always offering much needed encouragement along with incisive criticism and excellent advice, both in terms of content and organization. Our many hours of endless discussions have taught me a great deal about linguistic theory and have had a lasting influence on me as a scholar.

I would finally like to extend my gratitude to Juliette Blevins and Sam Al Khatib. Their questions and criticisms have challenged and pushed me to spell out as clearly and as fully as possible the theoretical assumptions and methodological procedures of CS linguistics, which many linguists are not familiar with.

# List of tables

# List of figures

CHAPTER 1

# The problem, methodology and theoretical background

## 1. Introduction

Why do speakers choose to utter *look*? Why, for example, do speakers choose *look* – but not *see* – for the communication of (a) message partials involving visual activity (*she looked at me*); (b) message partials involving attribution or judgment (*she looks tired*); and (c) message partials involving visual features (*it's the new look*)? In all these cases, is it the same linguistic unit '*look*' that is being chosen? Further, what motivates speakers to use *look* both for visual messages (*look at the picture*) and for intellectual messages (*look at the problem*)? Again, do these two cases present the same unit *look* or different *looks*? Yet more questions: Why do speakers combine *look* – but, again, not *see* – with (a) *for* in communicating a message partial of searching (*look for*); (b) *forward* in communicating a message partial of anticipation (*look forward*); (c) *up to* in communicating a message partial of admiration (*look up to*); and (d) *after* in communicating a message partial of care (*look after*), among many other combinations? Why, further, do speakers sometimes say *look me in the eye* but not *see me in the eye*, or *look at me* but not *see at me*? And why does *look* co-occur with *at* (*look at*) significantly more frequently than it co-occurs with *on* or *in* (*look on, look in*), though all three sequences occur many times? (*Look at* is of course most frequent, yet the question here is *why* this is so). And why do speakers use *look* even when the message involves nothing that is visually perceived (e.g., *looked into space*)? Lastly, why do people sometimes talk of a person's *look* and sometimes of a person's *appearance*? Why, for instance, do people *rely on looks* but *keep up appearances*?

Perhaps any linguist who became curious about *look* would have come to ask such questions – yet I propose that the answers provided here, and the theory of language in which they are framed, offer a fresh and novel contribution. In addition to these questions, many peculiarities in the distribution of *look* such as the following – all highly statistically significant tendencies found in the *Corpus of Contemporary American English* (Davies 2008) – have only just been discovered – as well as explained – through the meaning hypothesis for *look* that will be proposed in the present work: (a) *look* favors co-occurrence with a preceding *but* in comparison to a preceding *and* (☺ *but look...*; ☹ *and look...*) despite the fact that both sequences occur many times in the corpus;[1] (b) *look* favors co-occurrence with *this* in comparison to *the* (☺ *look at this...*; ☹ *look at the...*) again though both sequences are found many times in the corpus; (c) *look* favors co-occurrence with *carefully* in comparison to *carelessly* (☺ *looked carefully...*; ☹ *looked carelessly...*) though both combinations are found to occur; (notice that classifying *look* as an 'activity verb', as others have done, cannot explain this favoring, both modifications being equally applicable to activities); (d) *look* – in comparison to *see* – favors co-occurrence with *turn to* (☺ *turn to look*; ☹ *turn to see*), despite both sequences occurring many times in the corpus; (e) *look* – in comparison to *seem* – <u>dis</u>favors co-occurrence with *at the time* (☺ *seemed... at the time*; ☹ *looked... at the time*), both sequences of course found in the corpus; and finally, (f) *look* – in comparison to appear – disfavors co-occurrence with a following *but* (☺ *appears... but*; ☹ *looks... but*), both sequences occurring in the corpus, too. What is the explanation for these and many more, clear and strong, and newly discovered tendencies?

The central thesis of this research is that *look* represents a monosemous sign whose hypothesized meaning provides a unified explanation for why this sign's hypothesized signal – /lʊk/ or *look* – occurs where it does in texts, as perceived in both qualitative and quantitative distributional facts of the sort just described. Anticipating the fuller presentation of the meaning hypothesis in the chapters that follow, we can describe the meaning of *look* here using the shorthand formulation ATTENTION, VISUAL.

Guided by the overarching assumption that the structure of language is best revealed when it is taken to be an instrument of communication, the problem of this research is construed in terms of human speech/writing behavior; that is, we seek to explain why speakers utter *look* on each particular occasion. The solution is given in terms of the hypothesized meaning that is posited as a unitary invariant semantic value of the sign *look* that consistently motivates the choice to utter this sign's signal.

The meaning hypothesis will be elaborated and made precise in Chapter 2. But it is worth noting here that the proposed meaning is intentionally sparse in content. Among other things, the hypothesized meaning that we have summarized as ATTENTION, VISUAL underdetermines: (a) whether the message concerns an act of visually attending or attention-grabbing visual features (e.g., *He looked*

---

1.   None of the sequences mentioned here are regarded as ungrammatical or incoherent in any way. The smiling and frowning faces point to no more than facts of statistical tendencies.

vs. *his look*); (b) whether the Entity in Focus with respect to *look* (roughly, what is traditionally called a subject) is an agent exercising its visual faculty or an object of attribution (e.g., *He looked outside* vs. *He looked good*); (c) whether or not the message involves a visual stimulus being perceived (e.g., *He looked at the picture* vs. *He looked into space*); and (d) what the purpose of the visual act is, e.g., whether it is to search (*He looked for his glasses*) or to inspect (*He looked to see that everything's in order*), or something else. While the hypothesized semantic value of *look* is sparse, it will be shown to provide precisely the right amount of semantic substance that is necessary to explain all these different uses of *look* and more, as well as to explain why *look* is chosen where *see*, *seem* and *appear* may initially appear to be plausible alternatives. Indeed, the sparseness of the hypothesized meaning provides crucial explanatory strength that allows for this single meaning to explain by itself all occurrences of *look* without the need to invoke either polysemy or homonymy; that is, without positing multiple senses of *look* or multiple *look*s.

Confronted by the widely diverse distribution of this form, it may seem that *look* must have multiple senses (e.g., a visual sense and an intellectual sense), or that there is more than one *look* each with its own meaning (e.g., one '*look*-verb' and another '*look*-noun'). But positing multiple *look*s seems necessary only if one identifies the meaning of a form directly with a component part of the communicated message – an assumption that is not made here; instead, as we shall see soon below, meanings contribute to, but are not necessarily parts of, messages. We first turn to an exposition of the opposing position, followed by our position.

Identifying the meaning of a form with the message it is used to communicate.

Linguists from virtually all schools of thought are accustomed to identifying the encoded meaning of a linguistic form with some aspect – be it propositional or conceptual – of the ongoing interpretive experience that accompanies the use of the form in real or imagined speech events. In other words, both formal and functional linguists speak of the meaning side of a form as if it were known to speakers – including, crucially, known to the analysts themselves – simply by virtue of the subjective experience of understanding communicative intents in utterances where the form is found. In both traditions, linguistically encoded meaning is thus regarded as available to introspection (see Otheguy 2002: Section 4).

In the generative tradition, it is common practice to break an utterance into its meaningful component parts, each of which is assumed to correspond to a fraction of the interpretation of the utterance as a whole. This is generally known as the *compositional* view of meaning, where the meaning of a sentence is seen as a function of the meanings of its component parts and the structural relations that obtain between them. As a consequence, a single morpheme may be assigned an indefinite number of distinct meanings, depending on how speakers interpret it within different utterances. For example, *look* in *his new look* may be assigned the meaning 'visual features' because, in this utterance, a fraction of the communicated message appears to involve visible physical or sartorial characteristics. By contrast, the meaning of *look* in *He looked outside* may be rendered as 'visual activity' because, in this utterance, a fraction of the communicated message appears to involve a visual exploratory act (see Landau and Gleitman 1985: 132–3). In the former case, *look* would be assigned to the class of nouns whereas in the latter it would be assigned to the class of verbs; Section 2 below will discuss extensively the issue of letting lexical form classes guide the identification of linguistic signs.

Cognitive linguists, for their part, posit constructions as symbolic linguistic units and can assign *look* quite a number of different meanings, depending on the interpretation of the putative construction in utterances where it occurs. For example, the meaning of *look for* in *looking for my glasses* may be rendered as 'search' because it appears that, in this utterance, the use of *look for* involves the communication of a message partial of searching. Or the meaning of *look up to* in *looks up to his boss* may be rendered as 'admire' because the use of *look up to* in this utterance appears to involve the communication of a message partial of admiration. The identification of linguistic meaning with the interpretation of utterances is also what underlies the analyses of linguistic meaning in terms of polysemy. For example, Sweetser (1990) cites *look* as a polysemous form that encodes two senses – visual and intellectual. The reason why the sense of *look* in, say, *Look at the picture* is taken to be different from its sense in *Look at the problem* is because the communication of the former involves a message element of vision while the communication of the latter involves a message element of intellection.

Thus, in the cognitive approaches, frequent sequences (such as *look for*, *look up to*) are posited to emerge as constructions – linguistically encoded form-meaning correspondences – as these sequences become cognitively entrenched in the speakers' minds; and similarly, polysemy emerges in the linguistic system as speakers become unconscious of their using a word in two different ways. The issue of letting such cognitive considerations guide the identification of linguistic units will be discussed extensively in Section 2 below.

When the meaning of a form is thus identified with the conceptual fractions of message or message elements that the form is involved in, an analysis in terms of polysemy or homonymy quickly becomes inevitable, because virtually all words are used in multiple ways; that is, all words are used for the communication of multiple messages. But if it turns out that, in the case of many forms, the meaning of the form does not encode the message but is instead best analyzed as no more than *a guide toward the inference* of certain messages or message elements then an analysis in terms of monosemy becomes feasible. To this view we now turn.

Distinguishing between *meaning* and *message*. Following the analytical tradition of the Columbia School of linguistics (henceforth, CS), founded by

William Diver, it is maintained here that there is a sharp distinction between *meaning* and *message*; that is, between, on the one hand, that which is part of the linguistic code – the invariant meaning that consistently accompanies a corresponding linguistic signal – and, on the other, the interpretation of the code – the ongoing subjective experience of messages or message partials (Contini-Morava 1995, Diver 1995 [2012], Diver 2012, Huffman 2001, Otheguy 2002, Reid 1991). Meanings are here seen as merely sparse notional fragments that do not encode messages, and that provide but hints, prompts from which message elements are suggested and communicative intents can be inferred. Rather than compositional, linguistic meaning is thus characterized as *instrumental*, that is, the meanings of forms guide the hearer, through a process of inference, towards the speaker's intended message (Huffman 1997). Whereas in the compositional view of meaning, sentences are fractioned into components, each of which must be accounted for by a particular part of the linguistic output, in the instrumental view the meanings of individual signals do not add up to sentential meaning or to the communicated message at any level.

In keeping with the instrumental conception of meaning, it is recognized here that a single signal may imply different message partials on different occasions of its use, but – by hypothesis – the meaning consistently motivates the choice of its corresponding signal. So long as the chain of inference from the hypothesized meaning to the message elements suggested in the course of communication can be made precise by the linguist, then message elements that are different from the meaning (e.g., in the case of *look*, 'search' or 'admire') are allowed, indeed – given the human ingenuity to make new uses of existing tools – even expected by the nature of the hypothesis.

The putative meanings alluded to above – 'visual features', 'visual activity', 'search' and 'admire' – are too closely identified with the message partials that are communicated on particular occasions; consequently, any one of these meanings – if treated as a hypothesis – would fail to provide a unified explanation for the full range of the distribution of *look*.[2] As will be shown in this manuscript, these message partials are all but interpretations – occasional inferences that are based on the linguistically encoded meaning of *look*, as well as of the forms surrounding it, but that themselves exist outside of the linguistic system. The task here is to demonstrate that the hypothesized meaning that we have for now summarized as ATTENTION, VISUAL consistently contributes to the interpretation of

---

2. This statement applies to the putative constructions as well; for example, *look up to* does not always contribute to a message partial of admiration (e.g., *He looked up to the top of the mountain*), as will be discussed in Chapter 2.

texts where *look* occurs, whether it is in *look up to, the new look, look beautiful, look at, have a look,* etc.

This chapter continues as follows. Section 2 addresses the problem of the identification of symbolic linguistic units, particularly, the problem of identifying the phenomena that fall under the responsibility of this account of *look*. Three approaches will be explored in this regard. The first two approaches identify linguistic units prior to the analysis of a particular form; they are what I have termed (a) the syntactic and (b) the cognitivist, where linguistic units are identified, respectively, on the basis of syntactic function (Section 2.1) and cognitive status (Section 2.2). The discussion in Section 2 will also present the third approach – the one adopted here – which admits of the existence of a linguistic unit only following successful formulation of a meaning hypothesis. This section will thus make precise the place of CS in the field of linguistics, explicating its unique characteristics relative to both generative and cognitive grammars, including, in particular, why and how analysis in CS begins without assuming any a priori linguistic categories. Section 3 will then lay out the methodology that will be used in the qualitative analyses and quantitative predictions of subsequent chapters. Finally, Section 4 is a preview of what is to come in the subsequent chapters.

## 2.    The problem of the identification of linguistic units

Putting it first in the simplest terms, the hypothesis proposed in this manuscript is intended to explain why speakers say or write *look* on each particular occasion that this word is used, including why they say *look* in contexts where *see, seem,* and *appear* may initially appear as plausible alternatives. Going a little deeper, however, it soon becomes evident that the form *look* might represent, or be a part of, more than one linguistic unit.[3] Is there, for instance, one '*look*-verb' and another '*look*-noun'? Furthermore, are frequent sequences such as *look at, look for, looks like, looking forward to,* etc. independent linguistic units – each constituting a separate signal (construction) with its own unique meaning – that exist over and above the single signal-meaning pairing *look*? What we see from these questions is that the identification of the signal is just as much of a problem as the identification of its meaning, and consequently, both the signal and the meaning – the sign in its totality – constitute hypotheses.

---

3.    The term *linguistic unit* is consistently used in this chapter to refer to symbolic linguistic units, that is, form-meaning correspondences. Meaningless phonological units and purely formal grammatical structures are not intended.

Other linguists, whose position diverges from the one taken here, have talked about *look*, explicitly or implicitly, as if they knew in advance of analysis that this form represents multiple linguistic units, that is, multiple signals with multiple meanings (see e.g., Gruber 1967, Swan 1980, Landau and Gleitman 1985, Levin 1993, inter alia). There are two reasons why linguists might assume prior to analysis that there exist more than one *look*, the first reason being applicable to almost any linguistic school of thought, the second applicable specifically to cognitive linguistics. First, most linguists operate within a theory that allows for the a priori differentiation of linguistic units on the basis of the traditional grammatical categories (e.g., noun, verb, etc.). Second, cognitive linguists identify linguistic units with any seemingly cognitively stored linguistic representation that can be superficially seen as a form-meaning pairing. The next two subsections examine in detail each of these two reasons for positing more than one *look*; Section 2.1 addresses the syntactic motivation and Section 2.2 the cognitive motivation. The discussion of the cognitive motivation will address the possibility of polysemy, too; that is, it addresses the possibility that *look* represents one linguistic unit that nonetheless has more than one semantic value encoded in the language; (that *look* is associated with more than one value in the inferred messages is of course clearly recognized here). As we review these other approaches, we will present and defend our approach, according to which linguistic units are identified in response to successful analyses that hypothesize a stable and consistent relationship between a piece of form (a signal) and a piece of content (a meaning).

## 2.1  The problem of identifying linguistic units based on syntactic categories

A cursory examination of any dictionary will quickly reveal that there are at least two separate entries for *look* – *look v.* and *look n.* (e.g., OED Online 2015). In linguistic analyses, too, the distinction between these two *looks* is always at least implicit. Gruber (1967: 943), for example, states that *look* "is *obligatorily* Agentive", and concludes therefore, that "*look* is in *all* circumstances substitutable by the phrase *do something*, as are all Agentive verbs" (emphases, N.S). In the same vein, Landau and Gleitman (1985: 67) talk about "the verb *look*, which describes perceptual exploration", a notion characterized as one of "engaging in perceptual activity" (1985: 80). If *look* is substitutable by *do something* in all circumstances and, if its meaning has to do with engaging in perceptual exploration, this entails that in cases such as *It's the new look* or *You look tired* the form *look* must represent a different signal than the one that these analysts have in mind.

Further, even as a verb, it is quite common to talk as if there were two different *looks*. Swan (1980: 367), for example, states that "*Look* has two meanings.

One of them is similar to *appear* or *seem* [...] In this meaning, *look* is followed by adjectives, not adverbs. [...] The other meaning of *look* is related to seeing. [...] In this meaning, *look* is used with adverbs." And again, in the same vein, Levin (1993: 187–8) semantically classifies *look* once as a 'stimulus-subject-perception-verb' (along with *feel, sound, taste*, etc.) and then also as a 'peer-verb' (along with *peer, gape, leer*, etc.). Finally, 'peer-verbs', Levin states, are "not used transitively", a statement which entails the positing of yet another *look*, seeing as there are the admittedly somewhat infrequent but nevertheless well documented cases where *look* is used transitively (as stated in traditional terms), for example in *I looked him in the eye*.[4]

What we see is that the identification of the signal is regularly guided by syntactic categories that are accepted as established givens (see Diver, Davis and Reid 2012 for a thorough discussion). The linguists mentioned above are accustomed to talking about nouns and verbs as if these could be directly read off the data, that is, as if they were observational categories, but – as will be argued presently – they cannot, and are not.

The purpose of assigning lexical stems to formal syntactic categories is to account for distributional facts (see, e.g., Haegeman 1994: 37–38); for example, *look* occurs with nominal morphology (e.g., *the*) *because* it belongs to the category N. But in English, the vast majority of the lexical stems that occur with nominal morphology also occur with verbal morphology.[5] If almost any lexical stem in English can be assigned to the category N by virtue of its co-occurrence with morphology such as *the* or *a* then the category N does not explain the distribution of the stem, but simply captures the fact that the lexical stem has sometimes been found to co-occur with certain grammatical forms (like *the*) and is interpreted in a certain 'entity' type of way whenever it does.

A formal analyst may argue that the presence of nominal morphology is how one recognizes the category N. But notice that recognition can only take place for entities known to exist prior to their observation. The upshot is that if the analyst does not posit nouns prior to engaging in linguistic observation – that is, if N is not an a priori category – then nouns are not recognized. Strictly, all that one

---

4.  Gruber (1967: 942) similarly states: "*look* cannot be used transitively".

5.  Pierce (1985) reports a study of 30,000 words of running text from which all lexical stems occurring with verbal morphology and all lexical stems occurring with nominal morphology were taken and listed; in the end, 90 percent of the two lists were identical. Ten more similar studies, all based on actual texts published in magazines in 1959, show an average of 80 percent of identical lexical stems among the two lists. This study is cited in Reid (1991: 313).

recognizes is certain entity/thing interpretations that are regularly associated with the presence of certain morphology (like *the*).[6]

Meaning rather than form classes as the explanation for distributional facts. The decision to posit N and V as purely formal categories amounts to deciding prior to analysis that certain distributional facts have no semantic explanation. That is, that speakers can say, e.g., both *the look* and *looked* because *look* is assigned the categories N and V, these particular distributions having nothing to do with the unique lexical meaning of *look*. But these distributional facts do not, it turns out, require the postulation of syntactic constructs in the linguistic system because the same distributions – and many novel ones, too – can often be explained in terms of the meanings of the forms involved (see Otheguy, Rodriguez-Bachiller and Canals 2004). This will be demonstrated throughout the present work regarding the distribution of *look*.

Let's briefly consider how a meaning analysis can handle the fact that, while *look* regularly co-occurs with both *the/a* and *-ed/-s*, *see* on the other hand tends to occur for the most part only with *-s* and in the forms *saw* and *seen*. The reason speakers choose *look* for both entity and event interpretations while *see* is mostly chosen for event interpretations has to do with the specifics of the hypothesized meanings of both signs, as well as the expressive alternatives that exist for *see* but not for *look*.

Specifically, we first recall that the meaning that will be proposed for *look* – summarized in shorthand form here as ATTENTION, VISUAL – is neutral with respect to entity or event interpretations, while the meaning that will be proposed for *see* – summarized here as EXPERIENCING VISUALLY – specifically favors an event interpretation. This hypothesis for the meaning of *see* acknowledges that speakers have the option of choosing *sight*, a form not studied as part of this research but whose meaning (perhaps VISUAL EXPERIENCE) may be similar to that of *see*, only

---

6.    Entity/thing interpretation is not a theoretical construct; it refers to the interpretation of a lexical stem that has been shaped by its co-occurrence with grammatical forms such as *a* or *the*, whose meanings imply reference to a thing; (for example, the meaning of *the* – DIFFEREN-TIATION REQUIRED AND COMPLETE – contributes to a message partial involving a discrete – or differentiated – entity; see, e.g., Reid 1991: 79). By contrast, the term event (which is used soon below) refers to the interpretation of a lexical stem that has been shaped by its co-occurrence with other grammatical forms such as *-ed*, whose meaning implies reference to a time. The meaning of *look* is open to either thing- or event-like interpretations. For example, the co-occurrence of the meaning ATTENTION, VISUAL with the meaning DIFFERENTIATION REQUIRED AND COMPLETE suggests a message partial involving attention-grabbing visual features (e.g., *the new look*). Note that it is the meaning of the grammatical form *the* that contributes here to the lexical stem *look* being interpreted as a thing – i.e., as visual features as opposed to a visual event.

explicitly favoring an entity interpretation. When speakers want to conceptualize visual experience as a thing, they are likely then to choose *sight* (e.g., *I couldn't stand the sight of him*) because the meaning of *sight* more closely fits the intended message partial. *Look*, by contrast, is not in competition with a closely related form whose meaning differs only in that it specifically favors an entity interpretation, and so, speakers will choose *look*, by hypothesis, whenever the semantic substance of visual attention is at issue, whether the intended conceptualization involves a temporal act of visually attending or attention-grabbing visual features.[7]

Formal lexical classes as a solution of last resort. The CS approach does allow for the possibility of formal lexical classes, provided that no purely semantic solution can be found to solve the distributional facts at hand. In other words, positing form classes is a solution of last resort that would admit that certain distributional facts are synchronically arbitrary as far as the meanings of the individual forms involved are concerned. For example, this seems to be the case in Latin where lexical stems tend to occur either with verbal or with nominal morphology but not with both. In this case, positing form classes is a solution to a distributional problem that is observable prior to setting up these classes (Reid, CS conference 2015). But for English, no CS analysis to date has needed to posit nouns and verbs to solve distributional problems.

In this study, then, the data will not be seen through the filter of the traditional grammatical categories. Recognizing that these categories constitute hypotheses, not observations, we do not know in advance of analysis whether these hypotheses help solve the problem under study (Diver 1995 [2012], Otheguy 2002), in this case, the problem of why speakers utter *look* where they do. If the explanation for why *look* occurs where it does can be achieved by positing just a single *look* (which is neither noun nor verb, neither transitive nor intransitive) then that is the better hypothesis because it posits less while maintaining explanatory power, and further, as in the present work, because it leads both to testable predictions and to the discovery of new patterns of co-occurrence in written and (transcriptions of) spoken texts.

The starting point of analysis without the traditional a priori categories. In beginning analysis without a priori categories, the first step is, as suggested above, to keep well in mind that the observations give us no nouns or verbs, no subjects

---

7.  Another example where two closely related forms seem to constrain the use of one another is *appear* and *appearance*. While this requires further investigation, it seems that in general when we have a form A (like *see*) and a form B (like *sight*) that have essentially the same meaning with the exception that form A specifically favors event interpretations while form B specifically favors entity interpretations, then the use of form A will be constrained by the availability of form B to event-type messages.

or predicates, no sentences, indeed no linguistic categories of any kind. Rather, as Saussure wrote, "A language thus has this curious and striking feature. It has no immediately perceptible entities" (Saussure 1916 [1986]: 105). In the Saussurean tradition to which CS theory is heir, the linguist thus aims to start from a clean slate, assuming in language no discrete units in advance of analysis. This point is stated most strongly in the writings of Diver, who proposes that linguists need to think of the observations as ultimately being simply the asymmetry of the sound waves that occur when people speak: "In any instance of what we informally recognize as speech, what determines the form taken by the sound waves we observe?" (Diver 1995 [2012]: 451)

Diver recognizes that the sound waves present utter chaos in that no phonetic sequence ever occurs more than once, and that human cognition enables us to compensate by perceiving what are actually different instances of phonetic material as recurrent phonological units: "In the material being confronted, a certain sound wave is present because a certain phoneme is intended" (Diver 1995 [2012]: 456). Diver then proposes that phonological hypotheses are necessary in order to state grammatical hypotheses with respect to (most) signs.[8] The 'clean slate' question for the linguist thus becomes, not one about the sound waves, but rather one about why the phonemes occur where they do. This question, Diver explains, has to be answered on two levels, only the second of which concerns the analysis here. At the first level – not pursued in this work – the question concerns the occurrence and ordering of phonemes within a morpheme. At the second level, the question is why the morphemes themselves occur where they do in the stream of speech or writing.[9] This manuscript offers a partial answer to the second question by proposing a meaning hypothesis that explicates why *look* occurs where it does, including, as mentioned, why *look* occurs as opposed to *see*, *seem* and *appear*.

In proposing this austere Diverian approach to the observations, it must be acknowledged that the utterances to be considered throughout this manuscript are filtered through my own and other speakers' interpretations of the sequences of phonemes intended in the course of speech; so, for example, if someone happens to pronounce the name *Luke* as /lʊk/, the hypothesis here does not see itself

---

8.  Some signals are not phonological as will be explained shortly below.

9.  It should be noted that, while morphemic analysis is often useful in formulating a sign hypothesis, morphemes have no theoretical status within CS linguistics. The crucial difference between a *morpheme* and a *signal* is that morphemes can be posited prior to the hypothesis of a specific corresponding *sememe*, whereas a signal cannot be posited without positing an invariant meaning for it. Morphemes thus may serve as no more than pre-theoretical, provisional signals.

responsible for explaining this occurrence because – despite the similarity in the observable sound waves and the interpreted sequence of phonemes – this is clearly not an instance of the hypothesized signal with the meaning ATTENTION, VISUAL. Still, the analysis begins from a clean slate as much as possible. In this research, both spoken and written data have been appealed to, where the spoken data has been transcribed. In effect, then, what this work aims to explain is why we see the sequence of letters *look* in written and transcribed spoken texts.

Finally, a limitation in Diver's reasoning needs to be noted. Diver speaks as if morphemes always decompose into meaningless phonemes, when in fact, there are numerous languages that have phonological segments that are meaningful (e.g., plural -*s* in English) and even meaningful features (e.g., palatalization in Japanese Mimetic forms; Blevins 2012: 285), and moreover, there are also morphemes that carry meaning despite not decomposing into phonological segments (e.g., the English positive and negative expressions [ʔʌ'hʌ] and [ʔʌ'ʔʌ], nasalized vowels and contrasting glottal stop not occurring generally in English; Blevins 2012: 289–90). While these cases must be acknowledged, and while they serve to temper the perhaps too-simple formulation in Diver, they do not present an insurmountable problem. CS aims to make sense of the phonological observations by explaining the choice to make use of a hypothesized signal in terms of its hypothesized meaning; so long as the signal can be recognized, it ultimately does not matter whether or not it consists of a single phonological segment or feature, or whether or not it decomposes into meaningless phonemes.

With this in mind, it is important to note that CS analyses have often involved hypotheses about signs whose signal is not a phonological sequence. In addition to signals that are phonological sequences, there are (a) zero signals, that is, signals expressed through the absence of sound in a particular position, and (b) positional signals that are recognized by word order. To give an example of each, a zero signal has been hypothesized in the English system of Entity Number that consists of two signals: -*s*, whose hypothesized meaning is MORE THAN ONE and, the absence of -*s* – a zero signal – whose meaning is ONE (Reid 1991; 2011). Second, word order has been hypothesized as a signal in the English system of Degree of Control – ranking the relative degree of control that participants exercise over bringing about an event – where the signals are expressed through the ordering of the notions of *Participant – Event – Participant* (e.g., *The dog–$_P$ bit–$_E$ the man–$_P$*). In this system, the *Participant* that precedes the *Event* has the meaning MORE CONTROL (*dog*, in our example), while the *Participant* that follows has the meaning LESS CONTROL (*man* in the example) (see Reid 1974, Reid 1991: 174–8, Otheguy, Rodriguez-Bachiller and Canals 2004, Huffman 2006). Note that there is no phonological sequence involved in signaling the meanings of the Degree of Control System and that speakers must infer when a word is intended as a participant and as an event. We will return to the Degree of Control System in the explanation of a quite salient distributional difference between *look* and *see* in Chapter 4, namely, that *see* regularly co-occurs with the Degree of Control System whereas *look* does not. For present purposes, it is enough to make the point that anything can be a signal, so long as it is something that speakers can recognize.

## 2.2    The problem of identifying linguistic units based on cognitive status

In usage based linguistic approaches (e.g., Sweetser 1990, Goldberg 1995, Bybee and Hopper 2001, Tomasello 2003, Langacker 2004, inter alia) the identity of linguistic units is largely based on cognitive status; any seemingly symbolic construct that can be conceived of as stored and accessed as a unit, that is, anything for which there is reason to believe that it involves some cognitive representation, is considered a piece of linguistic structure. This conception follows from the idea that each linguistic utterance one hears and processes affects one's stored linguistic representations, and that the sum of linguistic experience at any given moment forms the basis for one's linguistic categorizations (Bybee and Hopper 2001). A linguistic category is defined as a cloud of remembered tokens, or exemplars, that have been associated with some category label on the basis of similarities across any salient dimension (Bybee 2006). The implication is that linguistic units are not stable but rather constantly emerging in response to the experiences with language one has had up to a particular point in time. Section 2.2.1 explicates how this view can lead cognitive linguists to posit constructions of which *look* is only a part, and Section 2.2.2 explains how this view has led cognitive linguists to analyze *look* in terms of polysemy.

### 2.2.1    *The problem of stored sequences*

Usage based approaches posit, in addition to individual words and morphemes, constructions – amalgamations of words and morphemes – that are taken to be independent linguistic units that exist in the grammar over and above their component parts. This view is expressed in Goldberg (1995: 1) as follows: "*constructions – form-meaning correspondences [... –]* exist independently of particular verbs … [C]onstructions themselves carry meaning, independently of the words in the sentence." In the same vein, Langacker (2004: 21) writes that "grammatical constructions are all inherently meaningful". Bybee and Hopper (2001: 9) give an example, revealing that the emergence of constructions is dependent upon the frequency with which their component parts are uttered together, and that the identification of a construction is based on its cognitive representation as a unit: "Tokens of *I* in *I don't know, I don't think, I see, I want*, etc. are mapped onto the same [cognitive] representations. This does not prevent a strong link between

*I* and *don't* from also being maintained, as *don't* is the second most frequent item to follow *I* ('*m* is the most frequent)"; these frequent sequences are then referred to as "emergent structure" (2001: 10). As we see, any sequential combination of linguistic units that, due to the effects of frequency, is taken to be stored and accessed as also being a unit (e.g., *I don't*) is seen as a grammatical construction.

If the effects of frequency were to be studied with respect to sequences involving *look*, it is likely that highly frequent sequences such as *look for, looking forward to, looks like*, etc. would be treated as constructions, each with its own linguistically encoded meaning (e.g., 'search' for *look for*, 'anticipate' for *looking forward to*, etc.) that would exist over and above the meanings of the component parts of the sequence.[10] But even if these sequences are cognitively stored units (which may well be), there still remains the question whether these can be identified as *linguistic* units.

In the usage based approach, positing *look for* as a symbolic linguistic unit is based on the analyst's intuitions of what the meaning of the sequence seems to be, yet, importantly, it is not based on having treated the purported linguistic unit as a hypothesis, at least not as one that is intended to explain speakers' expressive choices, and that is open to testing and falsification. If it were treated as a hypothesis (e.g., signal – *look-for*, meaning – SEARCH), it would have to be shown that the notion of searching invariably contributes to the interpretation of texts where *look for* occurs, and moreover, that this aspect of the communicated message cannot be attributed to the semantic contributions of *look* and of *for* when these occur independently of one another. This last point is crucial because, if the message elements that appear when *look for* is used can be explained solely in terms of the independent contribution of the meanings of *look* and of *for*, then there is no reason for positing an additional linguistic unit *look-for* on top of the units *look* and *for*; that is, the hypothesis for *look-for* would have no greater explanatory power.

Distinguishing between a cognitive unit and a linguistic unit. Note that it is perfectly compatible with CS theory to recognize the cognitive status of frequent sequences, as well as the effects of frequency on processes of grammaticalization and the rise of new units that have been studied in the usage based approaches. For instance, the word *breakfast* was presumably sometime in history a sequence of two signs, but it is almost certain that today's speakers recognize it only as a

---

10.   In Chapter 5 we will review in detail an analysis of the construction *have a look* posited in Wierzbicka (1988), and show that the meaning proposed for this putative construction does not stand to empirical testing. No other construction involving *look* has actually been analyzed in the literature, to my knowledge. Nonetheless, the putative construction *look for* will be discussed here below and again in Chapter 2, and *look like* will be dealt with briefly in Chapter 4.

single sign, that is, speakers no longer recognize meaningful internal component parts within this sequence.[11] This would be a case where the effects of frequency have resulted in the emergence of a new sign. But because, as will be argued in Chapter 2, occurrences of *look for* in speech and writing can be explained in terms of the hypothesized meanings of *look* and of *for*, *look for* is not hypothesized to be a sign – even if it is quite plausible that it is cognitively stored as some kind of a processing or experiential unit.

The power of the meaning hypothesis to explain regular co-occurrences. While constructions of the type proposed in other functional approaches are not admitted here as linguistic units themselves, it is worth stressing that the analysis offered in this research goes to great lengths to explain why speakers regularly use *look* in combination with certain other forms – both with forms whose regular co-occurrence with *look* is well known (e.g., *look* with *at*), as well as forms whose regular co-occurrence with *look* has been discovered here for the first time (e.g., *look* with *this*). Indeed, the counts that will be presented in Chapters 3 and 4 all compare the relative frequency of *look* with certain other forms, and the hypotheses proposed (for *look* as well as for *see*, *seem* and *appear*) offer an explanation for these regular co-occurrences in terms of the semantics of the individual forms involved. It is doubtful that many of the regular patterns that have been discovered through the hypothesized meaning proposed here would have ever been noted, much less explained, by approaches whose interest would likely extend only to the high frequency sequences involving *look*. The power of the proposed meaning hypothesis to discover and explain why relatively low-frequency sequences regularly recur is a crucial explanatory difference between CS and the usage based approaches.

Finally, note that even for the highly frequent sequences that are likely stored and accessed as units, there still remains the question – not addressed by the usage based approaches – of *why* the forms that make up the sequence came to be used together so frequently in the first place. In the usage based literature it is explicitly acknowledged that what causes certain sequences to recur frequently has to do with the meanings of the individual forms in the sequence: "My hypothesis is that semantics, and to some extent, pragmatics and our experience with the world, will determine what elements tend to occur together in sequences in an utterance, but repetition is the glue that binds constituents together" Bybee (2002: 11). Trivially, for a sequence to be stored as a unit it must first be the case that speakers have

---

11.  In other words, the hypothesis for *breakfast* as a monosemic sign (if we had one) would at some point in time offer a better explanation for the choice of this form than would the independent hypotheses of *break* and of *fast*, each as a monosemic sign.

already used it frequently. Speakers do not utter something *because* it is stored as a unit or because it has been frequently repeated, but rather, they do so because they want to achieve some communicative effect; the meaning of each individual form in a sequence explains why it occurs where it does, including why it regularly occurs with certain other forms. For Bybee, the question of what these meanings are and why speakers put those meanings together is set aside. But, because a CS analysis is specifically concerned with identifying explanatory symbolic units, it is well equipped to answer the question, seemingly logically prior to Bybee's account, of why speakers sequence certain forms together in the first place.

Significantly in the acquisition literature as well, Tomasello acknowledges that children must somehow learn the meanings of individual words before they can go on to learn the more abstract syntactic patterns that he postulates and studies. His research, however, has yet to undertake this endeavor, because, as he explains, "at the moment, the issue of how best to characterize children's early word meanings is unresolved" (Tomasello 2003: 58). Perhaps the work of CS linguistics can aid in resolving this issue.

A stable synchronic grammar. A final difference between CS and the usage based approaches needs noting. Unlike many usage-based approaches, CS posits a stable synchronic state of the grammar where something either is or is not a sign, and admits of no in-between status. This is so because, given the goals of the CS analysis, a hypothesized sign either can or cannot explain the occurrences of a signal in terms of its hypothesized meaning. The advantage of this position is that it makes the theory highly constrained, and individual hypotheses concerning the identity of signs and their meanings clearly falsifiable. In the usage based approach of, for example, Bybee, a sign, or a construction, as well as its meaning is not a stable unit, but one that is ever changing or emerging in response to usage events; indeed, the symbolic value of a sign in these approaches may be no more than the sum of its uses (see, e.g., Tomasello 2003: 100). It may very well be that if the goal is to explain the emergence of constructions through the effects of frequency, it does not matter so much whether signs are clearly identified units with rigid boundaries. But for the goal of CS of explaining speakers' choices and the resulting distributions by positing pairings of signals and meanings, the fuzzy boundaries proposed by the usage based approaches do not offer enough of an opportunity to falsify the hypothesized emergent units.

### 2.2.2    *The problem of polysemy*

Analysis of word meaning in terms of polysemy has been proposed in cases where a word has multiple communicative functions (as virtually any word has) and, importantly, the speaker is not conscious of the fact that the word is being used in different ways. In more recent times, one central avenue that has been posited that leads to polysemy is *conceptual metaphor*, a concept whose consequences on the analysis of *look* will be explored in detail in Chapter 2. Briefly, conceptual metaphor, as argued by its proponents, involves a mapping across two conceptual domains where people (unconsciously) see a similarity between two ranges of experience (Lakoff and Johnson 1980, Sweetser 1990). With respect to *look*, as well as other forms from the visual domain, a conceptual metaphor has been posited mapping the domain of vision to the domain of intellection (Sweetser 1990). This conceptual mapping is intended to explain why speakers use *look* both in *look at the picture* and in *look at the problem*, each case exhibiting a different sense of *look* (visual and intellectual, respectively).

The literature on metaphor explicitly acknowledges that the locus of conceptual metaphor is actually outside of language, that is, that metaphor is a fact of cognition generally rather than of language specifically (Lakoff and Johnson 1980, Lakoff 1993). It is nonetheless maintained, however, that, over time, metaphorical usage influences linguistic structure (see, e.g., Sweetser 1990). The effect of metaphorical usage on linguistic structure is *polysemy*, a concept involving the emergence of a structured interrelationship between metaphorical and non-metaphorical *uses* of a word – now promoted to the status of linguistically encoded *senses*. Sweetser (1990: 8) explains the admittance of metaphorically-linked polysemous senses into the linguistic code: "When a specific linguistic usage, based on [...] metaphorical structure, becomes no longer consciously metaphorical, then we can say that the linguistic form has acquired a metaphorically motivated secondary sense." Thus, *look* is taken to have evolved an intellectual sense, in addition to its visual sense (both senses forming a part of the linguistic unit *look*) because speakers are no longer conscious of the intellectual being a metaphorical usage.

The value of invoking conceptual metaphors in the course of linguistic analysis cannot be denied. But the appeal to conceptual metaphors for the purpose of justifying polysemy raises serious analytical problems. For example, a problem with positing two senses for *look* (one visual, one intellectual) linked by a conceptual metaphor is that there are many cases in which the communicated message simultaneously involves both vision and intellection. Examples with full discussion and analysis will be given in Chapter 2, but consider, briefly, *The doctor looked carefully over her notes*, where the doctor is simultaneously directing both her eyes and mind to the notes. Of course, from the cognitive linguistic perspective, fuzzy boundaries of this sort are expected. But, as noted above, here again, the fuzzy boundaries view comes very close to yielding an untestable hypothesis. This is so because, if the analyst is going to test a two-sense hypothesis (in this case a visual sense and an intellectual sense), then it must be possible to determine which sense the analyst is faced with on each particular occasion. This problem will be avoided here by explaining the use of *look* both for visual and intellectual messages in terms of a monosemous meaning that includes the notion of visual only. Once such explanation is achieved, there is no longer a reason for positing multiple senses.

Summing up the discussion of the cognitive approach, from a CS perspective, linguistic units are hypotheses intended to solve distributional problems, and so, cognitive status by itself provides no basis for positing a linguistic unit. CS analysts strictly distinguish between the linguistic code (an inventory of signs) and the cognitive effects that are a consequence of the use of the code, these effects including the cognitive storage and accessibility of sequences, as well as speakers' unconscious use of a sign for different messages, even messages that involve a conceptual metaphor. A sign is admitted as a properly linguistic unit only if it helps to solve a distributional problem, for which purpose the sign must be absolute, not fuzzy, so that its identification will be precise and its hypothesis clearly falsifiable.

## 3.  Methodology

In setting out to propose a meaning hypothesis for *look*, the first step is to closely examine the message elements that are produced by a great many texts in which *look* occurs to see whether some common semantic feature can be identified that justifies all instances of this sign's signal. The present work will offer analyses of both qualitative and quantitative data – all of attested occurrences of *look* – to support the hypothesized meaning, ATTENTION, VISUAL. The qualitative and quantitative methods of analysis will now each be explicated in turn.

### 3.1   Qualitative support

Qualitative support for the meaning hypothesis consists of analyses of attested occurrences of *look* within its linguistic context. In particular, we look for linguistic forms surrounding *look* whose semantic contribution appears to partially overlap with the hypothesized semantic contribution of *look*. These forms allow the linguist to get a handle on the message partial involved in the text under consideration without having to rely solely on intuitive understandings of what is being communicated. As a simple illustration of this analytical procedure, consider the following attested example.

(1)    We'll take a careful **look** at it and make a journalistic decision about
        whether to publish it.                                    (*ABC Nightline*)

First we note that the speaker in (1) uses *look* because the message concerns directing attention to the matter at hand (*it*) and, by hypothesis, ATTENTION figures in the meaning of *look*. Now the following pieces of contextual evidence support our hypothesis. First, while we do not have a meaning hypothesis for *careful*, it is safe to assume that this form contributes to a message partial of increased attention. The presence of *careful* thus (partially) supports the meaning hypothesis because both *careful* and the meaning of *look* harmoniously contribute to a message involving attention.[12] Further support in this short text comes from *make a journalistic decision*, an act which occurs as a result of looking. Making a decision involves conscious thinking and attention, and so, again, because ATTENTION figures in the hypothesized meaning of *look*, the presence of *make a decision* offers (partial) support for the hypothesis.[13]

The presence of forms with overlapping communicative effects provides a relatively objective means for supporting the meaning hypothesis, first, because these contextual features exist in the text independently of the analyst and of the hypothesis; and second, because these contextual features demonstrate that the hypothesized semantic contribution of *look* is present in the text independently of one's interpretation of just *look* (*careful* suggests a message element of attention, too).

Note that this phenomenon of using multiple forms to produce partially overlapping communicative effects is prevalent in texts because any given feature of a message (e.g., attention) will typically play a part in determining the speaker's choice of more than one linguistic sign (in Example 1, the suggestion of a message involving attention guides the speaker's choice of both *careful* and *look*). Consequently, the message elements to which each meaning individually contributes overlap, and reinforce one another (Reid 1991: 302).

The text in Example (1) offers support for ATTENTION only, and gives no support for VISUAL. The analyses offered here will focus mostly on supporting ATTENTION because VISUAL is taken to be rather more straightforward (in our present example, taking a careful look at the item mentioned is performed through the use of the sense of sight). Indeed, other hypotheses concerning the meaning of *look* that will be reviewed in Chapter 5 all posit visual in the meaning, while the notion of attention is unique to the hypothesis proposed here. Still, it is by no means

---

12.    Following Reid, "when two meanings jointly contribute to the communication of the same feature of the message [we may say that they] are in harmony" (Reid 1991: 304)

13.    Of course, *see* may also sometimes occur in close proximity to *decide/decision* despite the fact that the hypothesis to be proposed for *see* consists of no element of attention. In that case, the presence of *decide* will not be used to provide evidence in support of the meaning hypothesis for *see*, and other contextual evidence will be sought. Now, because both *look* and *decide* are chosen for a partially overlapping message effect while *see* and *decide* are chosen each for different and non-overlapping message effects, it may be predicted that *look* and *decide* will co-occur at a higher than chance frequency in comparison to *see* and *decide*. This prediction has been tested on background and has been confirmed.

trivial that VISUAL should figure in the meaning of *look* because there are many occurrences where no message element of visual is involved, such as in *look at your thought process*. Certain sections in Chapters 3 and 4 will therefore be devoted specifically to supporting VISUAL in the meaning of *look* through both qualitative and quantitative data. In brief, we will see that it is precisely because of the conceptual metaphor that maps vision to intellection that a meaning consisting of VISUAL alone can contribute to the suggestion of a message involving the intellect; in other words, there is no need to posit 'intellectual' in the code because the cognitive connection already exists in people's minds independent of the linguistic system.

It should lastly be noted that the methodology outlined above is quite different from the more familiar methodology of introspective judgments regarding sentences constructed by the analyst. In light of the goal of explaining speakers' expressive choices in actual speech/writing events, introspective judgments of such sentences are of little interest here. Furthermore, constructed sentences offer what would inevitably be a highly restricted dataset, limited just to those cases that the analyst could think of or, more crucially, that are of interest given the analyst's goals and assumptions. For instance, consider again the generative analysis of Gruber (1967) who states that *look* "is obligatorily Agentive"; his analysis is restricting the data just to those instances where *look* co-occurs with activity-suggesting morphology, and consequently, classifying the meaning of *look* as a type of activity becomes inevitable. In search for a hypothesis of an invariant semantic contribution for *look*, the dataset examined here has not been biased or restricted in any way.

## 3.2   Quantitative support

While the qualitative method of appealing to forms whose contribution appears to overlap with that of *look* is seen as a reliable and objective means for testing the meaning hypothesis, it may nonetheless still be argued that the analyst has manipulatively selected out of hundreds of examples specifically the ones that consist of these forms that supports their hypothesis. In other words, how do we know that examples such as (1) above are not just lucky? Quantitative tests are intended to address this doubt. More specifically, the purpose of quantitative testing is to establish the generality of a rationale that has first been proposed in the analysis of an individual example for a speaker's choice to utter *look*. All the quantitative predictions, therefore, will follow from a preceding qualitative analysis.

The quantitative method will be fully explicated in Chapter 3, but let's use Example (1) for just a brief illustration. Following the analysis of Example (1), we see that there is one shared reason – one overlapping communicative effect – that is leading the speaker to use both *careful* and *look*, that is, the suggestion of a message feature of attention. If it can be shown that Example (1) is representative of a regular pattern of the use of *look* and *careful*, that is, if the co-occurrence of the two forms proves to be favored in the corpus, then that will indirectly support the meaning hypothesis because it would argue that a notion that, according to the hypothesis, is contributed by the meaning of *look* (i.e., attention) has motivated its choice on multiple occasions. We say "indirectly support", because what the count is directly supporting is not the meaning – not the theoretical hypothesis, but rather the generality of the proposed reason for choosing the meaning – an empirical hypothesis. Choosing to use *look* and *careful* together to contribute to a notion of attention in the ongoing communication may be something speakers regularly do or it may not. If the count supports the hypothesis that they do, this argues that the one example analyzed was not just lucky, but in fact part of a larger distributional pattern. The co-occurrence of *look* and *careful* in the one example mirrors the regular co-occurrence of these two words in a huge corpus. The account of the example is thus not ad hoc. The same account is given for the statistical favoring of the two words.

In order to test whether the co-occurrence of *look* and *careful* is favored – that is, whether the two forms co-occur more frequently than the null hypothesis would predict – we must use a control term whose contribution to the ongoing message in no way involves the notion of attention (or visual), so that we can compare the frequency of *look* with *careful* to the frequency of *look* with the control term. The control term here will be *first*. Consider an example.

(2)    Coming up, a first **look** at the man who may have killed Paula.

(*NBC Dateline*)

In this example, *first* is used to suggest a message element of initiation or of something that has not occurred previously, whereas *look*, by hypothesis, is still chosen to produce a message element of visual attention. What is important is that there is no shared reason – no overlapping communicative effect – that motivates the speaker to use *look* and *first* together. Unlike *look* and *careful* in Example (1), here, each form – *look* and *first* – is chosen for reasons independent of the other and each produces completely different and non-overlapping message effects.

Following the analyses of Examples (1) and (2), it is predicted that *look* will favor co-occurrence with *careful* in comparison to *first*. To test this prediction the following searches (Table 1) have been carried out in the *Corpus of Contemporary American English*, henceforth COCA.

**Table 1.** COCA searches for *careful* and *first*

|            | Sequence        | Tokens |
|------------|-----------------|--------|
| Favored    | *a careful look* | 62     |
| Disfavored | *a first look*   | 109    |

And here are the results (Table 2).

**Table 2.** Total COCA occurrences of *careful* and *first* in the presence and absence of *look*

|  | *look* present | | *look* absent | |
|---|---|---|---|---|
|  | N | % | N | % |
| *careful* | 62 | 36 | 20469 | 4 |
| *first* | 109 | 64 | 549314 | 96 |
| Total | 171 | 100 | 569783 | 100 |

p < .0001

The prediction is confirmed. The right column of Table 2 (titled 'look absent') shows the baseline frequency of *careful* and *first*; the left column (titled 'look present') shows the prediction. The right side shows the number of all occurrences of *careful* and *first* except those where these words occur with *look*. Under these baseline conditions, that is, with no *look* to impact its distribution, *careful* represents only four percent of the *careful-first* total. Once *look* is introduced, however, *careful* skews in the predicted direction, accounting now for 36 percent of the total. A statistical test involving cross tabulation has produced a very low *p* value, indicating that the probability of the association between *look* and *careful* being due to chance is extremely low.[14] This data, therefore, confirms that speakers regularly use *look* to suggest a message feature of attention, and so supports ATTENTION in the meaning hypothesis. The confirmation of this and all the predictions presented below demonstrate through the use of a massive corpus that objective quantitative

14.   A chi-square, involving data of observed and calculated distributions, is used to produce the p-value. Note that the requirement of statistical independence – that is, that the occurrence of one (observed) token is independent from the occurrence of another – is reasonably met. This is so because the corpus consists of many thousands of different texts, independent from one another. The use of COCA is thus different from using, say, a novel as a corpus, because a novel is written by one person who possibly has a particular set of overall communicative goals. Indeed, Davis (2002) explains that the reason that CS quantitative counts have not traditionally been able to offer independent data points in quantitative counts is because the skewings observed in a particular text may be due to the particular communicative purposes of that text, and so there is no guarantee that another text will not be different. But in COCA, because each count spans thousands of different texts, we cannot point to any broad contextual element or communicative goal that is common to all. Still, however, the use of a p-value in this context is questionable since it is not clear in what sense precisely COCA can be seen as a representative sample of a larger population. Strictly, the use of the p-value is erroneous if no statistically legitimate inference can be made from the results in COCA to any texts outside of it. The favorings in this and the rest of the tables in this book apply only to COCA as it was in 2015.

evidence can be brought to bear on the analyst's interpretation of a particular example, either supporting it or failing to support it.

It is worth pointing out that, in Chapter 3, we will see another quantitative test demonstrating that *look* and *carefully* also co-occur at a higher than chance frequency. The fact that *look* regularly co-occurs with both *careful* and *carefully* is but one strong indication that the notion of attention contributes to the interpretation of texts where *look* occurs regardless of whether its surrounding morphology is what is traditionally called nominal (e.g., *a/the*) or verbal (e.g., *-ed/-s*).

Note lastly that, while the meaning hypothesis gives rise to quantitative predictions and consequently uncovers novel distributional patterns, the purpose here of offering quantitative data is not to predict the distribution of *look*, but rather to *explain* it. To this end, *careful* in our example above functions as a surrogate for a message element of attention, and its regular co-occurrence with *look* is explained due to the presence of ATTENTION in the hypothesized meaning. Because the predictions produced by this research have come out of an unbiased and unrestricted dataset, they have resulted in the discovery of many clear and strong distributional tendencies that have never been noted, much less explained, before.

## 4. Preview of upcoming chapters

The next three chapters consist of analyses of attested occurrences of *look* to support the meaning hypothesis, the fifth chapter reviews competing hypotheses of the meaning of *look*, and finally, the sixth chapter offers a discussion of the contributions of this study to CS analytical tradition. Briefly, of the three analysis-chapters, Chapter 2 is qualitative, Chapter 3 is quantitative, and Chapter 4 is comparative. In a few more words, Chapter 2 develops in detail the meaning hypothesis for *look*, and thoroughly demonstrates the explanatory power of the hypothesis in accounting for the wide array of this sign's uses through qualitative analyses of attested occurrences of *look*. In addition to explaining why speakers choose *look* for the communication of various different types of messages, Chapter 2 will also explicate how a meaning hypothesis for *look* that posits VISUAL for all its occurrences can explain the use of *look* for both visual and intellectual messages.

Chapter 3 continues to support the hypothesis, now through large-scale quantitative predictions that are tested through the use of COCA. The chapter will begin with a thorough explication of the quantitative methodology that has been adopted for this study, that is, that each quantitative prediction follows from a particular qualitative analysis proposing one shared reason – one overlapping communicative effect – that motivates the use of both *look* and another form. This inductive rationale for the regular co-occurrence of forms will be contrasted with a deductive rationale claiming to explain regular co-occurrences directly in terms of the compatibility of the hypothesized meanings. The reasons for adopting the inductive rationale and rejecting the deductive one will be explained. The chapter will then proceed to support the hypothesis through numerous quantitative counts, first, focusing on ATTENTION, and then, on VISUAL.

Chapter 4 offers meaning hypotheses for the forms *see, seem* and *appear* and explains why speakers sometimes choose each of these forms in contexts where *look* may initially appear as a plausible alternative. Doing this is an integral part of an analysis of *look* because it serves to account for constraints on the distribution of *look* that cannot be explained in terms of the meaning of *look* alone. The chapter consists of both qualitative analyses and quantitative predictions that compare the use of *look* to that of each of these other forms and explicates how each sign's respective meaning is responsible for creating its unique distributional patterns.

Chapter 5 then reviews three previous analyses of the meaning of *look*: one is a generative proposal presented in Landau and Gleitman (1985), another is a constructionist proposal presented in Wierzbicka (1988), and the third is another CS proposal presented in Tobin (1993). These competing hypotheses should be seen as indications that the meaning proposed here is by no means obvious or trivial. The discussion of these other hypotheses is postponed until the end because, only following the full presentation of the current hypothesis will the reader be able to evaluate its advantages and compare it to others.

Finally, Chapter 6 discusses the contributions of this study to CS linguistics, including, in particular, the discovery that a CS meaning, normally applied only to the domain of grammar, can be made applicable to lexical forms, too. The implications of this study to the lexicon-grammar distinction will be discussed in detail.

CHAPTER 2

# ATTENTION, VISUAL as the explanation for the choice of *look*

## 1. Introduction

This chapter argues that the hypothesis of a sign whose signal is the phonological sequence /lʊk/ and whose meaning is ATTENTION, VISUAL successfully explains the full range of this sign's attested distribution in terms of speakers' expressive choices. The meaning of *look* involves two notions, the first of which, ATTENTION, expresses a conceptualization of a state of mind, while the other, VISUAL, expresses a conceptualization of the physical sense of sight. Together, the two notions make up a single semantic substance, which may be more fully stated as *allocated mental resources focused by and directed through the visual track*. It is important to stress that the notion of visual attention is offered as a unitary meaning hypothesis; that is, *look* is hypothesized to have a single meaning involving a particular sensory-mental semantic substance. The notion of visual in the hypothesized meaning is shared by other forms – including *see* – whose precise meaning will be outlined in Chapter 4; the notion of attention is probably shared by other perceptual forms that have not been studied here, such as *listen*. The combination, however, of the notion of visual and that of attention within a single meaning (that consists of nothing more) is, by hypothesis, unique to *look*. This is thus a monosemic analysis of *look* that invokes neither polysemy nor homonymy. The hypothesis is summarized in Figure 1.

| Meaning | Signal |
|---|---|
| ATTENTION, VISUAL | /lʊk/ or *look* |

**Figure 1.** The hypothesis for *look* as a monosemic sign

While the proposed meaning may strike some readers as a straightforward observation that is hardly in need of validation, that impression is deceptive. The proposed meaning is a hypothesis, not an observation. We will see in this and the following chapters that the hypothesis of ATTENTION, VISUAL, precisely as formulated and with neither more nor less detail, is the only one that can provide an explanation for the many peculiarities in the distribution of *look*. Indeed, while the meanings offered by other linguists for *look* all involve VISUAL, different notions have been proposed to accompany it, including EXPLORATORY (Landau and Gleitman 1985) and PROCESS (Tobin 1993). While such hypotheses may all appear plausible, each is quite different, and the explanatory power of each is different, too. These discarded hypotheses will be examined in Chapter 5, after the presentation of the current hypothesis is complete. By then it will be evident that EXPLORATORY and PROCESS fail to explain many of the distributional patterns of *look* that have now been discovered specifically through the hypothesis of ATTENTION.

Throughout this chapter and the next two, the hypothesized meaning will elucidate numerous facts about the distribution of *look*, many of which were unknown before this research. We will come to understand why *look* is sometimes used in the absence of any visual sensory input; why *look* is sometimes used, and sometimes not, for what may at first appear to be essentially the same message; why *look* is used for messages of searching, either with or without a following *for*; and why *look* is used for messages involving the communication of an attitude or a state of mind. Finally, this chapter will deal with cases where instead of visual perception the communication concerns rather only the intellect. An extensive discussion of the well-established notion in cognitive-functionalist analyses of *conceptual metaphor* will be offered in connection with these uses of *look*. It will then further be demonstrated that a clear-cut dichotomy between visual and intellectual messages is impossible to sustain; instead, one finds a continuum of cases where metaphorical and non-metaphorical interpretations cannot be clearly distinguished. In the next chapter, we will show that the hypothesis leads to a substantial number of discoveries regarding clear-cut but previously unknown statistical tendencies of co-occurrence between *look* and other words and phrases in corpora.

Explanation versus description. In connection with the proposals outlined above, we stress that this account offers an explanation of the distribution of *look*, not a description of it. To understand the difference, consider what appears within a dictionary entry of *look*. The following are just a handful of the dozens of definitions provided for *look* by the Oxford English Dictionary (OED Online 2015).

a.   To direct one's sight (*He **looked** at me*)
b.   To direct one's gaze in a manner expressive of a certain thought or feeling (*The lion **looked** at Alice wearily*)
c.   To ascertain by visual inspection (*They open the book and they **look** if your name's on it*)

d. To direct or apply one's mind; to turn or fix one's attention or regard; to engage in mental contemplation, investigation, examination, etc. (*The situation, whichever way he looked at it, was uncomfortable*)

e. To expect, anticipate (*I am a pop punk solo artist looking to be signed to a label soon*)

f. To inspect, or peruse (*From time to time doctors came to shine penlights into his eyes and to look over his notes*)

g. To seek, search for (*She looks around for a food vendor*)

h. To have the appearance of being, to seem to the sight (*She looked like a monument planted there*)

i. The action or act of looking (*Those hoping for a look at the institution's vast collection of coins, textiles and other cultural artifacts will be disappointed*)

j. A person's (or animal's) appearance, especially that of his or her countenance (*Morden had the look of a schoolboy who has pulled off a glorious prank*)

What these entries show is that dictionaries provide a wide range of quite detailed message types where *look* can be found, without giving a unifying explanation underlying all its uses. There is no denying that *look* can be used for a wide range of messages, but the hypothesis proposed here goes beyond the description of usages in that it offers a unified reason for why *look* is used in all the different ways that it is.

To further appreciate the explanatory nature of the hypothesis proposed here as opposed to the descriptive account offered by the dictionary, let's see what happens if we treat the dictionary definitions as if each were a separate explanatory hypothesis concerning the meaning of *look*. In order for these hypotheses to be tested the analyst would have to be able to determine which *look* is being confronted on each occasion. But even a cursory examination of the definitions above reveals that this would simply be impossible. Let's take just one case to illustrate this point: definition (f) – 'to inspect' with its example *doctors came to shine penlights into his eyes and to look over his notes*. Now how could this 'inspect-*look*' (definition f) be distinguished from the 'apply-one's-mind-*look*' (definition d), for aren't the doctors inspecting their notes while putting their minds to attending to them? And further, how could this be distinguished from the 'direct-one's-sight-*look*' (definition a), for aren't the doctors directing their sight to the notes, too?

The hypothesis proposed here can by itself explain the use of *look* in all of the examples offered under these different dictionary entries, because the notion of visual attention fits the message being communicated in each and every one of them. The fit of the hypothesized meaning to the many different types of messages suggested by *look* will be explicated throughout the chapter. But briefly, note, for instance, that the act of visually attending to something involves orienting one's eyes in the direction of the stimulus attended to; this is why *look* is used both in *he looked at me* and *the lion looked at Alice wearily*. Notice that the portion of definition (b) which says 'in a manner expressive of a certain thought or feeling' has to do with the use of *wearily*, not with *look*. The dictionary is at fault here for mistakenly attributing something in the context (*wearily*) to the word that is being defined (*look*). As another brief illustration, consider the fact that visually attending to something is a volitional act, often motivated by some specific purpose, such as to ascertain or to inspect or to find something, etc. – through the use of the sense of sight; this is why *look* is used in *They open the book and they* **look** *if your name's on it,* **look** *over his notes* and *She* **looks** *around for a food vendor*. Notice here too that definitions (c), (f) and (g) – 'to ascertain', 'to inspect' and 'to search', respectively, have to do with the purpose of visually attending to something – a contextual feature not attributable to any one individual word, including *look*.

The dictionary treatment, much like many linguists, assumes that one can explicate the meaning of an individual word based on its interpretation within a given utterance. A central problem with this approach is that, if one attempts to define a word on the basis of its interpretation, then it is difficult (perhaps impossible) to determine precisely which message elements of the gestalt interpretation come specifically from the individual word in question, leading thus to misattribution, as has been illustrated above. To avoid misattribution, it is necessary to examine a great number of utterances consisting of *look* in an attempt to see whether a single contribution can be identified that is constant across all utterances in which this form occurs. If such a consistent contribution is identified, then it provides the explanation for why the sign *look* occurs where it does.

The fact now needs reminding that *look* can be used for messages involving either an act/occurrence in time or a kind of thing; putting it in traditional terms, *look* can receive both verbal and nominal interpretations. In the account proposed here, however, neither of them is inherent in its meaning. In the examples provided in (a-h) above, *look* functions as what is traditionally called a verb, that is, as an act taking place in time. But note that the suggestion of a message concerning an occurrence in time comes not from the hypothesized meaning of *look* but from the meanings of the grammatical forms that occur in its surroundings, such as *-ed*, *-0* or *-s*. Following Huffman (1989), and broadly speaking in accord with the grammatical tradition, these forms bear temporal distinctions, where, for instance, in *She looked*, it is hypothesized that the *-ed* following *look* means PAST. But the grammatical forms surrounding *look* may also be *the* or *a* – signifying information concerning the differentiation and identifiability of entities (see e.g., Reid 1991: 77–80); or they may be *-0* or *-s* – signaling information concerning the Number of entities, that is, singular or plural (Reid 1991: Chapter 2). When *look* occurs with any of these entity-suggesting grammatical forms then ATTENTION,

VISUAL is construed as a thing rather than an occurrence in time. The reader may be accustomed to thinking of noun and verb as separate lexical categories, but there is every reason to believe that the meaning ATTENTION, VISUAL fits the message regardless of what grammatical forms co-occur with *look*. The examples presented below intersperse noun and verb uses without distinguishing among them.

Turning to a quick reminder now regarding qualitative methodology; throughout this chapter, analyses of attested occurrences will demonstrate that message partials involving the notion of visual attention are consistently suggested by the use of *look*. Such a demonstration relies on contextual evidence against which the meaning hypothesis is tested and, either supported or rejected. In particular, the analyses below rely crucially on the presence of particular forms in the text that independently show, without appealing to the analyst's or the reader's intuitions or apprehensions of the message, that the notions of visual and of attention are present wherever *look* is used. For a brief illustration, consider the following attested utterance.

(2)   … **looking** at one spot of attention…                         (*MBSR YOGA #1*)

In this case, the presence of *one spot of attention* straightforwardly suggests that a message partial of attention is at issue in this text, thus supporting ATTENTION in the hypothesized meaning of *look*. VISUAL does not find support in this short linguistic context, but the extra-linguistic context unambiguously indicates that the addressee is instructed to direct their vision to a spot of attention. While it is necessary to show that both VISUAL and ATTENTION consistently contribute to the interpretation of messages where *look* occurs, the analyses to follow concentrate mostly on demonstrating that attention is a relevant feature of the message, given that visual is in most cases much more straightforward.

Finally, wherever relevant, the analyses here and in the next two chapters will appeal to aspects of the phenomenology of visual attention in humans as studied by psychologists. As will be demonstrated, the following phenomenological aspects of visual attention (summarized in Hatfield 1998) prove relevant in explaining the distribution of *look*: (a) narrowing of the visual field and the clarity of visual stimuli, (b) the active directing of the eyes and mind, (c) temporary fixation of the eyes and mind, and (d) involuntary shifts of attention. These phenomenological aspects are distinct from the meaning hypothesis, and should not be taken as implying multiple senses of *look*. Rather, because in deploying the meaning ATTENTION, VISUAL, speakers likely associate it with these experiential aspects, an appeal to them can sometimes facilitate our understanding of a speaker's motivation to use *look*.

The rest of this chapter is structured as follows. Section 2 briefly examines the most straightforward use of *look* for messages concerning acts of visual attention.

The subsequent sections explore and explain the less straightforward uses of *look*. The fit of the hypothesized meaning with message partials where a visual stimulus is absent is discussed in Section 3; the fit with message partials involving the communication of one's thoughts or feelings is in Section 4; the fit with message partials involving attention-grabbing or attention-worthy visual features is discussed in Section 5; the fit with message partials concerning visual attribution is discussed in Section 6; the fit of the meaning with messages of either visual or intellectual attention is discussed in Section 7; the fit with message partials of searching is in Section 8; finally, Section 9 discusses both the visual and intellectual uses of *look* in combination with the directional terms *up, down, forward, back* and *after*.

The types of messages alluded to above by no means exhaust the uses of *look*, and not every use of *look* will fit neatly within one of these categories. In presenting the examples below under separate sections I am not positing a hard and fast taxonomy of usage types. The classification of uses is made purely for presentational purposes and has no theoretical import. Every occurrence of *look* is equally motivated by the hypothesized meaning, and no claim is made that there exists a discrete or finite number of message types associated with *look*.

## 2.    The fit with messages involving acts of visual attention

The first example provides clear-cut evidence for the hypothesized meaning.

(3)    [Yoga instructor:] Twist the body to the right, as you bring your right arm behind you, […] twisting the head and **looking** as far to the right as you can, even **looking** into the far right corners of your eyes, finding a spot to focus on and keeping your attention there as best you can. This helps to improve concentration and focus.
        (*MBSR YOGA #1 – https://www.youtube.com/watch?v=_pYoDdUijY8*)

In this example, the instructor chose *look* (as opposed to, say, *see* or *stare*) because the message involves an act of visual attention. This is evidenced, first, by the use of *your eyes*, supporting VISUAL, and by the use of *finding a spot to focus on and keeping your attention there*, supporting ATTENTION.

Deepening the analysis, Example (3) nicely illustrates how the different aspects studied by psychologists in the phenomenology of visual attention play a role in explaining the use of *look* in terms of its hypothesized meaning. First, it has been noted by Hatfield (1998), relying on a much older tradition in the psychology of visual attention, that there is an inverse relation between the intensity of attention and the cognitive material that can be brought under it: "the greater the attention, the smaller the part of the visual field to which it extends" (1998: 5). In example (3), the use of both *spot* (indicating a visual stimulus that is as narrow as can be) as well as *focus* provide evidence – independent of the use of *look* – that the message here concerns a narrowing of the visual field, thus supporting ATTENTION in the hypothesized meaning. Second, visual attention is experientially associated with an act of voluntarily orientating one's eyes toward the direction of attention (Hatfield 1998: 9). In Example (3), *to the right* and *into the far right* provide evidence of a message partial that involves actively orienting one's eyes, thus again supporting ATTENTION. Third and finally, visual attention is also experientially associated with the human ability to choose to sustain one's attention while retaining the eyes fixed toward one visual stimulus (Hatfield 1998: 11). In Example (3), the instructor says *keeping your attention there*, where the use of *keeping* suggests a message partial of fixation, again supporting the hypothesized meaning.

One may argue against us, as we have argued above against the dictionary, that it is these other forms (*eyes, spot, attention, focus, to the right*) that are responsible for suggesting a message involving visual attention, and that this notion in the message has mistakenly been attributed to *look*. If the hypothesis relied on just this one example, then such an argument would certainly be in order. But, throughout this chapter and the next two, we will see that the notion of visual attention invariably accompanies texts where *look* occurs (even in the absence of contextual support).

## 3.   The fit with messages where a visual stimulus is absent

The meaning ATTENTION, VISUAL may be used for messages that involve the active directing of the eyes (here, *into space*) irrespective of whether or not there is a visual stimulus to be perceived. This is so because, by hypothesis, the meaning of *look* only involves attention that is directed through the visual track, saying nothing about the reception of visual sensory input; the meaning of *look* thus leaves it to contextually-based inference whether such input is or is not part of the message.

(4)   Maureen did not answer but sat on the bench **looking** into space. Her thin lips were pressed flat together in a way that made her seem heartless. I wondered if she felt the need to maintain her authority or if she simply didn't want to involve herself in my problems. Or perhaps she thought I was ranting and was deliberately ignoring me.                    (*Quiet People*)

*Look* is used in Example (4) because the message involves Maureen actively orienting her eyes. The purpose of orienting her eyes into space is not to perceive anything, but rather, as the context makes evident, to avoid her interlocutor by deliberately directing her visual attention away from him (*deliberately ignoring me*).

Note that the sparseness of the hypothesized meaning is what enables a straightforward explanation of such examples; any hypothesis that went beyond ATTENTION, VISUAL and proposed a meaning that included the reception of a visual stimulus would not be able to account for cases like this one. In Chapter 4, the meaning of *look* will be compared to *see*, whose meaning hypothesis does involve a visual stimulus, impacting thereby its unique distribution, as will be shown.

### 4.   The fit with messages involving the communication of one's thoughts or feelings

Consider first the following expressions, all attested.

(5)   The eyes are the windows to the soul.

(6)   We have no need to speak. We communicate with deep soulful **looks**.

(7)   **Look** into my eyes and hear what I'm not saying, for my eyes speak louder than my voice ever will.

Example (5) does not feature *look*, but it is a well-known expression reflecting the fact that people consider the eyes to be a reliable source of information concerning a person's thoughts and feelings. Because people sometimes communicate their thoughts and feelings through visually attending to one another, the meaning of *look* can be used for messages involving such acts, as demonstrated in Examples (6) and (7). These examples do not provide much context, but Example (8) below offers plenty of contextual evidence that supports the hypothesized meaning.

(8)   [A list of suggestions for successful courting:] Lock eyes. According to David Givens, PhD, a direct gaze triggers powerful physiological responses, such as increased heart rate and brainwave activity – two things that also happen when he's turned on by you. Hold his gaze for about 8 to 10 seconds. That's the ideal length of time to make eye contact with a guy, and men are most responsive to long, not short, glances. The scientists found that the more you share a **look**, the more attracted to you he'll feel. Then you have to glance away. Because you are **looking** at him and then averting your eyes, this hard-to-get type of eye contact subconsciously triggers him to want you even more. In fact, this is Mother Nature's best man-magnet tool. In the animal kingdom, it's called a copulatory gaze, and it will definitely appeal to your man's primitive instincts.

(*Cosmopolitan* – *Touches that Lock Down His Love*)

The meaning of *look* has been chosen in this example because the message concerns communicating through the eyes (*eye contact*), an act which requires attracting the other person's attention and holding their gaze so that the person recognizes your intent. This attending with one's eyes thus explains why the meaning of *look* has been chosen as opposed to, say, *glance*, which may also suggest actively turning one's eyes, yet not specifically with attention. Note the linguistic evidence available in the text. First, *lock eyes* and *eye contact* clearly indicate that the message involves the sense of sight, thus supporting VISUAL; second, *lock*, *contact* and *hold his gaze* indicate that the message involves the eyes being intently fixated, thus supporting ATTENTION.

Speakers can use the meaning of *look* to conceptualize that communication which one transmits through one's gaze (e.g., *gave her a look of surprise*) because the meaning of *look* may contribute to a message that involves one's eyes communicating through their intent direction and fixation toward someone else. Consider the following attested example.

(9)    I looked at Elaine and she narrowed her eyes and gave me a **look** that said 'go to hell'.                                                        (*The Bachelor Party*)

The narrator uses the meaning ATTENTION, VISUAL because the message involves Elaine intently directing her eyes toward the speaker, not in order to perceive him but rather to communicate something (*go to hell*) with her eyes. Evidence in support of the hypothesis is found in *narrowed her eyes*, supporting both VISUAL (*eyes*) and ATTENTION (*narrowed*).

## 5.   The fit with messages involving attention-grabbing visual features

This section explains the fit of the meaning of *look* for messages involving attention-grabbing or attention-worthy visual features. Take, for instance, the expression *the new look*; the reason why *look* is used here is to suggest that the visual features in question – often in regard to fashion – are the ones that now catch the public's attention. Let's turn now to the following attested example.

(10)    Models Toni Garrn (left) and Karlie Kloss show off one of the season's most stunning trends backstage at Dior: perfect red lips paired with a luminous complexion. Makeup artist Pat McGrath painted models' mouths with Cover Girl Lip Perfection Lip-color in Tempt, Hot, or Flame ($6.50 each), a **look** she hails as "refined, modern, and elegant."
(*Harper's Bazaar magazine*)

*Look* (as opposed to, say, *appearance*) is chosen because the message involves the visual features attained through the application of lipstick, a product that is expressly designed to draw visual attention to its wearer. Note the linguistic evidence that supports the hypothesis. First, the models *show off* the new lipstick, suggesting that its visual features are interesting and attractive and capture people's attention. Next we find the descriptive terms *stunning, perfect red* and *luminous*, all of which are strong accentuated visual properties clearly intended to grab people's attention. Lastly, the names of the available lipstick colors are quite suggestive themselves, being called *Tempt, Hot* and *Flame* – all names that unequivocally bring out the fact that the visual features achieved by using this product are intended to attract attention.

The next example involves a person's inherent, attention-grabbing visual features; the hypothesized meaning explains why *look* is attested here, too (again, as opposed to *appearance*, which might have been a plausible alternative).

(11)    "When I was growing up, they called me La Prieta Fea – the Ugly Dark One. I'm the darkest one in the family. But I actually think it helped me develop a personality. I couldn't rely on my **looks**."

(*Esquire*: The complete guide to women 2005)

The speaker uses *look* because she is contrasting between her attention-grabbing visual features (*my looks*) and her internal personality traits (*develop a personality*). VISUAL is trivially supported by the contrast between her external and internal features. ATTENTION is supported by the suggestion that she couldn't *rely on* her visual characteristics. To rely on one's visual characteristics would suggest that one accrues some benefit from other people due to one's visual features. Now, if these features are going to affect people's actions and behavior toward one then one's visual features must be noticed and attended to. Indeed, note that the speaker's visual features were attended to and did influence people's behavior toward her (leading people to call her *the Ugly Dark One*); only these features were thought to be negative, so they did her no good. Thus, the use of *rely on* suggests that the message concerns attention to visual features and *look*, as opposed to *appearance*, is chosen because the meaning of *look* is ATTENTION, VISUAL whereas *appearance*, as we will see in Chapter 4, has no element of attention in its meaning.

## 6.    The fit with messages involving attribution based on visual attention

Because people often make judgments of attribution on the basis of having visually attended to something (which, in turn, allows people to determine its properties), the meaning of *look* can be used to suggest message partials involving visual attribution, particularly when the message concerns the attention-worthiness of the attributed properties. As a brief illustration, by hypothesis, speakers will use *look* in the compliment *You look beautiful* rather than, say, *are* – *You are beautiful* – because the use of *look* suggests that the speaker has given attention to the addressee's visual features. Out of context, it may seem that in such examples *look* and *are* are (sometimes, at least) interchangeable, but the analyses in this section demonstrate that this is not so. The analyses below thus rely on the different decisions speakers make to use or omit *look* in what may at first appear as rather similar messages that are in fact, as we shall see, quite different. Let's begin with the following pair of attested examples contrasting the presence of *look* in *you look beautiful* (Example 12) to its absence in *you're beautiful* (Example 13).

(12)    You never want people to notice your accessories. When you walk into a room, heads should turn. The desired effect is for everyone to say or think that you **look beautiful**. If people comment on your shoes or bag, they're not appreciating the entire essence that is you. If you go to a museum and see a statue on a podium, you don't want people to say, "Wow, what a stunning podium. Where can I get one of those?" Your entire ensemble should be so captivating, so cohesive, that one particular thing can't be singled out. It supports you; you don't support it.          (*Harper's Bazaar*)

(13)    African-American parents must be especially vigilant, says Powell-Garlington, because some physical traits – dark skin, tightly coiled hair, thick lips – aren't as widely embraced by society, even by other blacks. "The more you affirm your kids' beauty and build their self-esteem, the more they'll internalize it" she says. Bettye Barber of Columbia, South Carolina, took this to heart when her daughter, 5-year-old Mikki, became upset over the fact that her bead adorned braids were too short to shake and clank like Zaria's, her 2-year-old sister, whose hair is shoulder length. "I had to do some fast talking" Barber explains. "I told her about how beautiful her hair is and how everybody has different hair lengths, and that when her hair is in its natural state, it's just like Mommy's." Of course you don't want to pile on the praise so much that your child can't keep her little ego in check. So it's also important to emphasize that beauty has a wide range. You might say to her, "Yes, **you're beautiful**, but so is she."          (*Parenting Magazine*)

The meaning hypothesis for *look* explains why it is used in (12) but not in (13). The message in (12) involves attention to visual features, as is amply supported by the presence of *notice your accessories, comment on your shoes, heads should turn,* and *captivating ensemble*. We see then that *look* is used in Example (12) because the speaker wants to communicate a message feature of attention, and ATTENTION is a part of the meaning of *look*.

In (13), by contrast, there is no evidence suggesting that the message concerns attention to the child's visual features. Note that, whereas in (12) the message involves a person's visual features on a particular occasion – a particular evening of a social event, the mother in (13) is reaffirming not that the child has beautiful visual features that the mother has noticed at that moment, but rather that the child's visual features are generally beautiful; that is, the mother is pointing to something intrinsic to the child, whether anyone is paying attention or not.

We turn now to another pair of examples involving attribution, and again compare the decisions to include and omit *look*, contrasting now *look like* to *be like*.

(14)   [Katie sees Peter after a long time they haven't met:] "You haven't changed much," she said. "You look a little thinner. It's becoming. You'll be very attractive when you're fifty, Peter." "That's not very complimentary – by implication." "Why? Oh, you mean I think you're not attractive now? Oh, but you are." "You shouldn't say that right out to me like that." "Why not? You know you are. But I've been thinking of what you'll **look like** at fifty. You'll have gray temples and you'll wear a gray suit – I saw one in a window last week and I thought that would be the one. (*The Fountainhead*)

(15)   I read an article that said every ten years we become a different person. It's easier to look back and say, "I'm so different than I was ten years ago," but it's so hard to look forward and imagine what you'll **be like** at fifty. Your entire life, you're evolving and growing and changing as a person.
(http://www.citypages.com/music/greycoats-if-our-last-album-was-molasses-this-ones-san-pellegrino-6629417)

*Look* is used in Example (14) because the communicated message involves the notion of visual attention, as evidenced by Katie's use of *I've been thinking* and *I thought*, indicating that she has consciously directed her attention toward Peter's visual characteristics (*thinner, attractive, gray temples* and *gray suit*). In (15), by contrast, the message concerns neither attention nor visual features, and hence the absence of *look*. Instead, the message in (15) involves a person's personality and character, as evidenced by *we become a different person* and *evolving and growing and changing as a person*.

It is worth finally pointing out that this phenomenon of using *look* when the person looking is not the Entity in Focus (roughly, what is traditionally called a subject) is by no means unique to *look*. It parallels the usage of such forms as *wash* or *read*, as for example in *Silk washes easily* or *This novel reads well*.[15] Both in the

---

15.   The distinction between forms such as *easy* and *easily* is outside the scope of this research. It may briefly be noted, however, that *This book reads easily* and *This book reads easy* – despite possible pressures of prescriptive grammar – are both found to occur in COCA (e.g., "This looks pretty good – **reads easy** as a book"), and seem to communicate rather similar messages. By contrast, examples such as, say, *He looked diligently* and *He looked diligent* clearly involve quite different communications. This difference between *look* and *read* in their interaction with forms like *easy* and *easily* may be explained by the fact that the meaning of *look* is suitable both for messages involving object attribution (e.g., *diligent*) as well as for messages involving

case of *look* and (presumably) in the case of these other forms, the meanings of the forms underdetermine the number of participants involved as well as which roles these participants might be playing in particular communications.

## 7. The fit with messages involving either visual or intellectual attention

The hypothesized meaning of *look* has been proposed in full awareness of one of the most difficult aspects of *look*'s distribution. In our view, the hypothesis can explain why this meaning is used for messages where no physical visual perception or visual features are at issue.

(16)   There is something about your decision making that is flawed and you need to **look** carefully at why this is the case.

(www.reddit.com/r/leaves/comments/2o0w96/<br>i_need_to_change_my_marijuana_habits)

To explain such uses of *look* a discussion of the notion of *conceptual metaphor* is first in order. Since the groundbreaking work of Lakoff and Johnson (1980) it has been recognized that metaphor is not merely an occasional poetic device, but rather that it is a central process of conceptualization, pervasive both in the ways people think as well as in the use of language. A conceptual metaphor is construed as a systemic correspondence or *mapping* between two conceptual domains where, typically, one is relatively concrete (the source domain) and the other is relatively abstract (the target domain).

   In the case at hand, the relevant mapping is the one said to link our physical experience of vision to the abstract domain of intellection (Lakoff and Johnson 1980, Sweetser 1990, Lakoff 1993 inter alia). The experiential basis for this conceptual mapping is the primary status of vision as a source of knowledge about the world (Sweetser 1990). This status, of course, is peculiar to humans; if we were more like bats then our experience might have led to a metaphorical mapping between auditory perception and intellection, but given the biological makeup of humans, sight is our primary source of information regarding physical objects. Indeed, studies in child language have shown that visual features play a crucial role in children's early discrimination of one category from another (Clark 1976). Note that while people do gain knowledge through auditory perception (primarily

---

action manner (e.g., *diligently*), while the meaning of *read* (though we do not know what it is precisely) seems suitable only for messages involving action manner. The consequence is that with *read* there is no potential for confusion whether *easy* or *easily* are used, whereas with *look* speakers use *-ly* to imply a message that specifically applies to an activity.

because of the use of language), sight is a far more useful sense for data gathering, simply because so many objects in the world do not emit stimuli audible to humans.

Another experiential basis – and one of particular interest with respect to *look* – regarding why people think of the abstract domain of intellection in terms of physical vision has to do with the highly developed focusing ability that is unique in humans to the visual sense. The ability to willfully focus or concentrate attention on one stimulus at the expense of others is a salient characteristic of both vision and thought (Sweetser 1990). None of the other senses, with the exception of hearing, allows for such voluntary control, and even hearing is less consciously and readily focused in comparison to vision. Humans have the ability to move their eyeballs at will from one stimulus to another, and further, even with the eyeballs remaining fixed, we can easily shift focus across different distances; suppose, for instance, that you hold a pencil in front of your eyes – you can readily focus your vision on the pencil, seeing it perfectly sharp, and then in an instant turn to focus your vision beyond the pencil, causing it to blur while the objects in its background sharpen. Vision is the only sense that allows for such skillful maneuvering and focusing. In this respect, our experience with vision is quite similar to our mental experience where we likewise have the ability to focus on mental and intellectual content and shift our attention from one thought to another at will.

The above has been a deductive explanation motivating the link between vision and intellection, yet there is, in addition, independent evidence in support of this metaphorical mapping. One of the strongest arguments found in the literature for the existence of conceptual metaphor is the fact that a conceptual link across two domains of experience spawns a whole family of metaphors that are pervasive throughout the language. When it is observed that an entire family of expressions from one domain are systematically used for messages in another domain then this strongly suggests that there exists an underlying conceptual link connecting the two domains. It is not only the word *look* that is used for messages involving both vision and intellection. Rather, there is a wide range of linguistic expressions in English whose meanings, though we may not have precise hypotheses for, nonetheless clearly have to do with the visual domain and yet are used to communicate messages concerning the intellectual domain, too. Consider: *see the problem, the mind's eye, keep her in the **dark**, shed **light** on the issue, **illuminate** the issue, **obscure** the issue, **spotlight** the important issues, be **blind** to her concerns, put her theory under a **microscope**, his ideas were just a **blur**, an **opaque** argument, a **transparent** conclusion, a **clear** concept, his **view** on the matter*, etc.

This phenomenon is not unique to English, either. Many languages likewise deploy words from the visual domain for messages in the intellectual domain

(Sweetser 1990). As one brief example, the Hebrew phrase *ra'a et ha-or*, which literally translates as 'saw the light', is used to convey a message of realization, a truth dawning on one.

Yet another piece of evidence for the cognitive link between vision and intellection comes from expressions such as *I saw it with my own eyes*, which conveys the utmost certainty in one's knowledge. Indeed, in many languages that have grammatical markers for evidentials, visual data is considered the most reliable, certain and objective kind of knowledge there is (Sweetser 1990: 33).

Having established that there is a conceptual link between vision and intellection we can return now to Example (16) (***look** carefully at why this is the case*) and explain it quite straightforwardly. The explanation for the use of the meaning ATTENTION, VISUAL in communicating this non-visual message is the conceptual connection between vision – which forms a part of the meaning of *look*, and intellection – which is a feature of the message being communicated. Thus, *look* is used because the writer is advising the addressee to direct their mental or intellectual attention, that is, to think *carefully* about their decision making.

It should be noted that the theoretical status of the cognitive metaphor is different from that of the sign *look*. The sign constitutes a unit in the linguistic code, whereas the metaphor is a way of thinking (Reid 2004). Indeed, while metaphor affects language, "the locus of metaphor is not in language at all, but in the way we conceptualize one mental domain in terms of another" (Lakoff 1993: 202–203). Once it is acknowledged that there exists a cognitive metaphor that maps the domain of vision to the domain of intellection, the intellectual use of *look* can be accounted for in a straightforward way in terms of this form's visual meaning. Treating the visual metaphor for intellection as a (linguistically relevant) way of thinking rather than a feature of the linguistic system proper in no way diminishes its importance; indeed it has a critical role in explaining many occurrences of *look*. Still, the cognitive metaphor has a different ontological status from things that are in the linguistic code – signs consisting of signals and their meanings – and it plays a different role in the explanation (Reid 2004).

Now some linguists may ask – why not explicitly build the intellectual value into the meaning of *look* so that the meaning would posit two paths of directed attention, one through the visual track and another through the intellectual track? In other words, why not give *look* two semantic values where each value would stand in a closer relation to the message it is being used to communicate?

The answer is given in light of the objective of this account, that is, to explain speakers' choice to use *look*. This explanation is given in terms of the contribution of the hypothesized meaning of *look* to speakers' intended messages. Note that this account is entirely explanatory, and not descriptive. A comprehensive description of the uses of *look* would treat the visual and intellectual uses on a par, as we see in the Oxford English Dictionary. But 'intellectual' is not posited as part of the meaning because the meaning is an explanation of the use of its signal – not a description of usages. And, because of the conceptual metaphor mapping vision to intellection, the meaning ATTENTION, VISUAL can explain the use of *look* for intellectual messages. In short, by the principle of Occam's razor, the reason why no additional semantic values are posited here for *look* is that more are not needed to explain its use.

Further and moreover, note that a polysemic analysis seems feasible only when the database is largely restricted. Thus, if the analyst only considers a handful of examples, some like *look at the picture* and others like *look at the problem*, then it may well appear that the uses of *look* fall neatly into discrete conceptual categories, one involving only vision and another involving only intellection. But as more examples are analyzed, the conceptual space between the various putative senses fills in, revealing a continuum that defies a principled partitioning. Thus, whereas it may seem that *look* concerns a purely visual message on some instances and a purely intellectual message on others, there are in fact many cases where the two are combined and blend into one another. The next two examples illustrate this point; first, example (17) shows a case where *look* suggests more of an intellectual message yet visual is involved, too; then example (18) is a case where *look* clearly suggests a message of visual attention and yet intellectual attention is part of the message, too.

(17)   I compared two books to see how they exercised their option in reference to *that*. The first was Captain Mahan's *The Influence of Sea Power upon History*, a very serious and learned treatise written in a high level of academic style. In the whole first chapter of this volume, the Captain does not once omit *that* when he might have. The level of precision is retained in respect to *that* as in respect to all else. Then I **looked** at a modern detective novel, one of the Nero Wolfe series, where the narrative is in the first person, and the narrator is a very breezy and informal individual, with language to match. He omits *that* about half the time, responding readily to variations in precision. His sound waves would be very different, in this respect, from those of Captain Mahan.          (*The Elements of a Science of Language*)

The writer has directed intellectual attention to particular aspects of the narrative and language of the book, yet, at the same time, he did so through directing his vision to the printed text. If a polysemic hypothesis were advanced as an explanation for the use of *look* then the analyst must be able to tell which *look* is being faced on each particular occasion. But determining whether *look* in this example is the visual *look* or the intellectual *look* seems impossible, for both notions are simultaneously part of the message (note that if the writer had examined the book through the auditory track then perhaps *listen* would have been used instead of *look*). The meaning proposed here explains this use of *look* without any need to decide between vision and intellection.

The next example nicely demonstrates that when people direct their attention to some visual stimulus it is often because they have an intellectual interest in that stimulus, and the act of attending to the stimulus visually is performed by way of examining it intellectually.

(18)   [Howard Roark, an aspiring architect, is introduced to the reader at the very start of the novel: standing on a cliff, observing the natural environment that surrounds him...] He **looked** at the granite. To be cut, he thought, and made into walls. He **looked** at a tree. To be split and made into rafters. He **looked** at a streak of rust on the stone and thought of iron ore under the ground. To be melted and to emerge as girders against the sky. These rocks, he thought, are here for me; waiting for the drill, the dynamite and my voice; waiting to be split, ripped, pounded, reborn; waiting for the shape my hands will give them.                                    (*The Fountainhead*)

While it is clear that Roark visually attends to these natural features, it is also clear that – at the same time – he directs his intellectual attention to them, too. This is indicated by the repeated use of *thought* that follow the occurrences of *look*, as well as by the fact that the message concerns active planning – an intellectual activity; that is, Howard has an intellectual interest in these natural features as he is going to use them in his architectural endeavors. What is important is that a clear-cut distinction between visual and intellectual messages is again impossible to make because attending to something visually may well involve attending to it intellectually at the same time. Indeed, it is worth pointing out that in the psychological literature it is noted that an act of visual attention involves the external directing of the eyes as well as the internal directing of the mind (Hatfield 1998); as an illustration, suppose you are perceiving a tree, and then directing your mind – through the visual track – to different parts of it e.g., to the leaves, or to the branches, or to the trunk, or to the shape of the tree or to its color, etc. (the illustration comes from Wolff 1738 § 256, cited in Hatfield 1998: 12).

Examples like (17–18) provide further empirical confirmation of the naturalness of the connection between vision and intellection, as they show that the cognitive metaphor plays a role even when there is physical visual perception involved, too; that is, these example confirm the conceptual connection between vision and intellection because both of these notions are simultaneously present in the messages communicated by these texts. Whereas a polysemic analysis (if treated as a hypothesis that is subject to falsification) would require the analyst to spell out which *look* it is on each particular occasion – the visual *look* or the intellectual *look*, the monosemic hypothesis can successfully explain – with, crucially, the aid of the conceptual metaphor – the fit of the hypothesized meaning to the message even when the message spans both the visual and intellectual domains.

## 8.    The fit with messages of searching

Perhaps contrary to one's initial assumption, the use of *for* following *look* is not a necessary condition for the suggestion of a message partial of searching produced through the use of *look*.

(19)    He **looked** around the airport, trying to find his friend, Alfred.
(http://artzyrainbow.deviantart.com/art/America-
x-Male-Reader-Gaming-Love-523092833)

In (19) there is *look* and there is a message partial of searching, yet there is no *for*. Still, the use of *look* can be explained in terms of its hypothesized meaning ATTEN-TION, VISUAL; *look* is used because the message concerns a person directing their attention, through the visual track, all around the airport.

Of course, a message partial of searching is often produced through the use of *look for*.

(20)    [Jack enters the house to check if his friends are there:] Jack **looked for**
Arlen, but didn't see her. He **looked for** Haley and Ric, but they were still
sitting on the pier.                                                        (*Ghosting*)

The question is what in the linguistic input is responsible for this message partial. There are at least two analytical possibilities. First, *look for* may be an unanalyzable unit (which one might want to spell *lookfor*) whose meaning is SEARCH, and that exists in addition to the hypothesized units *look* and *for*. Second, a message partial of searching may not be linguistically encoded but is rather inferred through the independent contributions of the hypothesized meaning of *look* and the hypoth-esized meaning of *for*, and in light of additional contextual features.

As regards the first possibility, if one were to posit SEARCH as the meaning of *look-for* then one clear advantage would be that that would offer a closer fit between the meaning and the communicated message in many cases, such as Example (20). But as indicated in the previous section, the account here is purely explanatory, not descriptive; if the single meaning ATTENTION, VISUAL can explain the use of *look* in these examples then there is no need to posit an additional unit of which *look* is only a part. Indeed, if the hypothesized meaning ATTENTION, VISUAL fits the message conveyed in (20), as will be argued soon below, then hypothesizing an additional unit *look-for* with the meaning SEARCH would result in an untestable hypothesis, for the analyst would not be able to determine in cases like (20) which of the two units it is – the ATTENTION, VISUAL *look* or the SEARCH *look-for*.

We are led then to the second possibility: the notion of 'search' is an emergent, contextually induced feature of the message that need not be attributed to any single linguistic component; that is, it is not encoded by *look*, or by *for*, or by the sequence *look-for*, but is rather an inference suggested by the use of *look* and of *for* in combination with contextual evidence.

To understand the inferential process leading to a message of searching, a brief explanation of the hypothesized meaning of *for* is in order. According to an unpublished paper by Alan Huffman, *for* signals a meaning that concerns the notion of reason. As a brief illustration, consider an example such as *I received a bill for $50*; if I received a bill for $50, Huffman explains, then the $50 I owe is the reason I received the bill. Similarly, in Example (20), Jack's friends are the reason he actively directs his attention through the visual track.

Now, how does this lead to a message of searching? As mentioned, it is clear from the context that Jack does not visually perceive his friends (*didn't see her*). Given that, if Jack's friends are the reason he engages his eyes in an act of visual attention, then, presumably, his act of visual attention is motivated by wanting to perceive them, leading to the inference that he is searching for them. Notice, finally, that here, too, it would be difficult to separate visual attention from intellectual attention; while Jack directs his eyes to various places around the house he also directs his mind to the task of finding his friends (this may be even clearer in cases such as *looking for a job*, used to describe the act of reading posts online or in a newspaper).

## 9. *Look* in combination with directional terms: *up, down, forward, back* and *after*

This section looks at some common expressions featuring *look* followed by a directional term, including *up, down, forward, back* and *after*. As demonstrated in the pairs of examples below, all of these sequences may be used either for messages involving physical visual perception (the (a) example in each pair) or for messages involving only the intellect (the (b) example).

(21)  a.   I turned slowly and **looked up** to the top of the castle wall.

*(The Remembering)*

  b.   I admired you! **Looked up** to you!          *(Red and Green)*

(22)   a.   You can **look down** at the floor or out over your fingertips.   (*Yoga # 1*)

     b.   The Catholic Church **looks down** on involvement in pornography.
                   (*Geographical Review: Religion in Sin City*)

(23)   a.   Crush heard another knock and **looked forward**. "There's a cub on my hood."                    (*Bear Meets Girl*)

     b.   It's so hard to **look forward** and imagine what you'll be like at fifty.
           (http://www.citypages.com/music/greycoats-if-our-last-album-was-molasses-this-ones-san-pellegrino-6629417)

(24)   a.   He would often **look back** to make sure he hadn't been seen.
                                    (*The Manipulator*)

     b.   It's easier to **look back** and say, "I'm so different than I was ten years ago"
               (http://www.citypages.com/music/greycoats-if-our-last-album-was-molasses-this-ones-san-pellegrino-6629417)

(25)   a.   She turned to **look after** him as he walked away.
           (*His Mother's son* - http://archiveofourown.org/works/925344)

     b.   [Said of a lion:] He did have a marvelous even-tempered, friendly nature and I think we just became part of his family like a pride of lions. He knew he was the center of the world and everyone was there to **look after** him.
               (*NBC Dateline: Amazing Animals Caught on Tape*)

First, regarding the (a) examples, the reason why *look* is used in these cases can be explained straightforwardly since these messages all involve actively orienting one's attention through the visual track, toward some specified direction. Now, in the (b) cases there is no message partial of visual perception and, moreover, the metaphorical mapping between vision and intellection is insufficient to explain the messages that are suggested by these utterances. Yet, by hypothesis, the contribution of *look* in each case is one and the same; *look* is used here every time because its meaning – ATTENTION, VISUAL – contributes to the communication of a directional message. In addition to the meaning of *look* and the metaphorical mapping of vision to intellection, we must appeal to the metaphorical mappings that are operative with each of the directional terms as well in order to explain the unique message partial suggested by each of the examples. The metaphorical mappings involved in the cases of *up* and *down*, as well as *forward* and *back* are quite well understood, while the case of *after* is somewhat less clear but can still be made sense of.

Beginning with *up* and *down*, two related metaphorical mappings have been posited that are relevant for the analysis of Examples (21) and (22). The first is GOOD IS UP, BAD IS DOWN; the second is HIGH STATUS IS UP, LOW STATUS IS DOWN (Lakoff and Johnson 1980; Lakoff 1993). In the case of (21), the message partial of admiration comes from the suggestion that the person to whom the speaker directs her attention is up above her; that is, because the speaker must direct their attention upwards, the implication is that the speaker thinks of the addressee as someone good, someone held in high regard, in short, someone to be admired.[16,17] In the case of (22), the message partial of disdain and contempt comes from the suggestion that the Catholic Church has to direct their attention downwards to pornography; that is, pornography is conceived of as bad, and held in low regard.

Turning to *forward* and *back*, these are spatial terms that are metaphorically mapped to the domain of time; future times are in front, past times are behind (Lakoff and Johnson 1980, Lakoff 1993). In (23), the speaker is expressing that it is hard to direct one's intellectual attention to the future and think what one will be like at fifty. In (24), the speaker expresses that it is easier to direct one's attention to the past and see how you have changed and developed.

The metaphor involved with *after* has not been studied, as far as I know. Still, we might consider other expressions that indicate that being physically behind someone is conceptually linked with protecting or supporting or taking care of them. Thus we have expressions like *I've got your back* and *I'm behind you whatever path you take*, both suggesting message partials of protection and support. In (25) then, the speaker conveys that the lion to whom the speaker and her family have directed their (intellectual and/or visual) attention is in front of them; that is, they are in a position from which they can protect and support it.

## 10.   Conclusion

This chapter has argued that the hypothesized meaning of *look* fits the wide variety of different types of message partials that are communicated through its use. Indeed, we have seen that the meaning is sparse and underdetermines the message yet it is sufficiently precise to be explanatory of the meaning's uses. Unlike the dictionary treatment of *look*, the hypothesis here has isolated the consistent semantic contribution of *look* proper, allowing for particular messages to be inferred from

---

16.   Many people must experience as children physically looking up toward the people that they look up to. Also, consider the architecture of, say, a Gothic church, where the height of the space seems often to trigger an action of physically looking up in awe and admiration.

17.   Further regarding *up*, this form is also sometimes used to imply that some activity was done in a very thorough way, one way being that it is done to completion; it can't be done more. For example, one may say *We're out of milk; I used it all up* (i.e., used it until there was no more); or *you're going too fast, wait up for me* (i.e., wait until I am no longer behind you); or *Downton Abbey will wrap up next season* (i.e., end). Similarly in *I looked the word up in the dictionary* – i.e., directed attention to the dictionary until the word was found.

the meaning of *look* as well as from the meanings of the forms surrounding it and any relevant aspect of the extra-linguistic context.

These are the various message partials to which the meaning ATTENTION, VISUAL has been shown to render itself useful. First, the meaning allows for communications that involve no visual stimulus being attended to, but rather only the active directing of the eyes. Second, ATTENTION, VISUAL, which gives no indication as to entities or events, can consequently be construed in the message either as an occurrence in time or as a kind of thing. Construed as a kind of thing, we have seen that the meaning of *look* enables messages involving the communication of one's thoughts or feelings through one's attending eyes, and also that the meaning of *look* can be used for messages involving attention-grabbing visual features; in Chapter 4 we will return to messages involving visual features when we compare the use of *look* to that of *appearance*. We have also examined why *look* is sometimes present and sometimes absent in messages involving attribution and have seen that *look* is used when the attribution is based on having given visual attention to something; in Chapter 4 we will return to messages of attribution and compare the use of *look* to that of *seem* and *appear*. This chapter has further argued that, because of the cognitive link mapping vision to intellection, the meaning ATTENTION, VISUAL can account for the uses of *look* that involve the intellect, too. It was argued here that there is no justification for positing two separate senses to *look*, first, because the account is explanatory rather than descriptive and a single meaning can by itself explain these non-visual uses; and second, because the visual and intellectual are quite often both features of the message and so a distinction of uses to purely visual and purely intellectual simply proves impossible. Finally, we have analyzed occurrences involving the combination of *look* with other forms, including *for, up, down, forward, back* and *after*, and have seen that, contrary to what might initially appear, none of these sequences has a single constant message effect with which it is associated. Still, throughout, the use of *look* has been shown to make the same consistent contribution in whatever context it appears.

The next chapter continues to motivate the hypothesized meaning of *look* through qualitative analyses that will lead to quantitative predictions. The quantitative data will demonstrate that the hypothesized meaning accounts for numerous large-scale distributional patterns of *look*, many of which have been discovered and are noted here for the first time.

# CHAPTER 3

# Using big data to support the hypothesized meaning ATTENTION, VISUAL

## 1. Introduction

This chapter continues to investigate how the hypothesized meaning ATTENTION, VISUAL impacts the distribution of *look*, now through large-scale quantitative predictions. These predictions will be tested through counts conducted over all occurrences of *look* in the *Corpus of Contemporary American English* (COCA). As will be explicated below, the quantitative predictions presented in this and the next chapter follow from particular contextual co-occurrences observed in the course of qualitative analyses. These quantitative predictions thus test the relative frequency at which *look* co-occurs with particular forms that will have already been observed to co-occur with *look* in the analyses of individual examples, and whose presence has been shown to support the meaning hypothesis for *look*. It is shown, for example, that modification of *look* by *carefully* – a form suggestive of a message feature of attention (e.g., *He looked carefully at the image*) – provides qualitative support for the meaning of *look*. Then, in order to provide quantitative support, it will be predicted that, even though sequences of *look carefully* and *look carelessly* both occur, *look* should co-occur with *carefully* more frequently than with *carelessly*. Or in another example, the modification of *look* by *with big eyes* will also be argued to offer qualitative support for the meaning hypothesis. Then, in order to provide quantitative support, *eye* will be used as the predictive term and *hand* as the control term, and the prediction will be that the combination *look-eye* should be more frequent than the combination *look-hand*. In these kinds of predictions that are advanced in order to provide quantitative support for the meaning hypothesis, items like *carefully* and *eye* are called the *predictive term* while items like *carelessly* and *hand* are called the *control term*. In this way, a quantitative prediction is designed to establish the generality of a rationale that is first proposed in the analysis of an individual example for a speaker's choice to utter *look*. The confirmation of such predictions offers objective evidence in support of the meaning hypothesis because it argues that the meaning accounts for features of the distribution of *look* (such as its relatively frequent co-occurrence with *carefully* or with *eye*) throughout a corpus.

Note that each quantitative prediction is constrained to test for only a single semantic parameter at a time. For example, the relatively frequent co-occurrence of *look* with *carefully* can only offer support for ATTENTION in the meaning of *look* but not for VISUAL; this is because *carefully* is only suggestive of a message partial involving attention but is not suggestive of a visual message. Similarly, the relatively frequent co-occurrence of *look* with *eye* can only offer support for VISUAL but not for ATTENTION; this time because *eye* is suggestive of a visual message but not of a message concerning attention. While each quantitative prediction zooms in on and isolates a single semantic parameter, the qualitative analyses will show that the choice to utter *look* is simultaneously motivated by both VISUAL and ATTENTION. A qualitative analysis is limited, however, in that it can only account for the occurrences of *look* on a case by case basis, whereas a single quantitative prediction can explain at once a great number of occurrences through counts conducted over all instances of *look* in a massive corpus.

This chapter consists of three main sections. Section 2 raises the problem of the rationale for the regular co-occurrence of forms in a corpus, and of what precisely is tested in making quantitative predictions; it lays out in detail the quantitative methodology adopted here. Sections 3 and 4 motivate the meaning hypothesis through qualitative analyses that lead to quantitative predictions, arguing that the hypothesized meaning successfully explains why *look* occurs where it does throughout the corpus. These sections have been divided on the basis of the semantic parameter supported through quantitative predictions. Section 3 presents quantitative predictions that involve ATTENTION, Section 4 presents predictions that involve VISUAL.

## 2.   Methodology

Two related questions must be answered with respect to the rationale given for quantitative predictions. One, what precisely motivates the regular co-occurrence of forms; and two, what precisely is being tested and what can predictions of regular co-occurrences affirm? This section will argue that regular co-occurrences can be predicted when a qualitative analysis has posited a shared reason that is motivating the speaker to utter the two forms together. The prediction, then, tests the generality of that reason – which follows from the hypothesized meaning – for uttering the two forms; the meaning hypothesis is thus indirectly supported, through the reason posited for its choice (Reid 1995).

In a bit more detail, we proceed from the underlying assumption that speakers choose to utter certain forms as these forms are expected to contribute to certain message effects; the expected contribution or effect on the message is seen as the reason motivating the speaker to utter the form. Taking the regular co-occurrence of *look* with *carefully* as example, one reason a speaker may have for choosing to utter *look* is – by hypothesis – to contribute to a notion of visual attention.[18] As it happens, this contribution partially intersects with the contribution to the message made by uttering *carefully*, because *carefully* is also chosen to contribute to the message a notion of attention. Thus, *look* and *carefully* are chosen (at least in part) for the same reason. Because the speaker's reason for choosing the meaning of *look* partially intersects with the reason for choosing *carefully* – both (in part) suggestive of attention – the two forms are expected to co-occur with greater than chance frequency. This rationale will now be developed in greater detail in Section 2.1 below; Section 2.2 will then address the justification for the inductive nature of this rationale.

## 2.1 Quantitative predictions test the generality of communicative strategies

In order to understand the methodological procedure leading from qualitative analyses to quantitative predictions an explication of the term *communicative strategy* is now in order. Following Reid (1995), a communicative strategy is a principle of choice motivating a speaker to utter a particular linguistic form in light of some message feature to which the form in question is expected to contribute upon its use.[19] In the case of *look* the claim is that speakers are motivated to use this sign in order to contribute to the message a notion of visual attention. The idea is quite straightforward; speakers choose a meaning that best contributes to their intended message, and so, the semantic substance that makes up the hypothesized meaning often constitutes the motivating factor that leads a speaker to utter that meaning's corresponding signal.[20]

Recall that each quantitative prediction isolates and tests for just one of the two notions present in the hypothesized meaning of *look*. In explicating the methodology below, the focus will be on the suggestion by *look* of a message

---

18.   Another reason to choose to utter *look* may be to contribute to the message the notion of intellectual attention, as has been discussed in Chapter 2.

19.   While this definition is taken from Reid, the notion of a communicative strategy is attributed to Diver and appears in several of his early writings, including *The Elements of a Science of Language* and *The Nature of Linguistic Meaning*, both of which now appear in Diver (2012), as well as in Diver's latest work *Theory* (1995: Section 3.4.4).

20.   There may also be indirect communicative strategies, that is, reasons for choosing the meaning that follow from – yet nonetheless are distinct from – the semantic notion that forms the substance of the meaning. For instance, as discussed in Chapter 2, another reason for choosing the meaning ATTENTION, VISUAL may be to suggest a message feature of intellectual attention, even though 'intellectual' does not figure in the hypothesized meaning of *look*.

feature of attention. Now, as has been amply demonstrated throughout the previous chapter, one prominent way to tell whether the notion of attention is a message feature in a particular utterance is by looking to the linguistic context in which *look* is used and checking whether there are other forms that might likewise contribute to a similar message effect of attention. Suppose, for instance, that *notice* is used in close proximity to *look*, as in (26).

> (26)    He [= Peter] tried not to **notice** the faces of the people he passed, but he had to **notice**; he had always **looked** at people.    (*The Fountainhead*)

In this example, the writer uses *notice* to suggest a message feature of attention; that is, Peter could not help giving his attention to the faces of the people he passed. In light of our (limited but sufficient) understanding of the semantic contribution of *notice* (defined with the words 'attention, observation' by Google dictionary), its use in the same utterance as *look* provides independent evidence that a message feature of attention is indeed at issue in this utterance of *look*. Thus, given the choice to use *notice* in the same context as *look*, we may conclude that the choice to utter *look* (as opposed to, say, *see* or *stare*) is likewise made in light of the suggestion of a message feature of attention.[21] The two forms, then, partially overlap in their communicative effects. That is, the choice to use *look* and the choice to use *notice* were each in its turn motivated – at least in part – by the suggestion of a similar notion of attention in the ongoing message.[22]

When in the course of the analysis of a particular example it is proposed that two forms are chosen for the same reason – as is the case here with *notice* and *look* – then the generality of this claim may be tested through a quantitative count; that is, we may predict that the co-occurrence of the two forms will be favored in the corpus. The rationale for the prediction is that if two forms are chosen to produce partially intersecting message effects then they have a higher than chance frequency of co-occurring than if each is chosen to produce completely different and non-overlapping message effects (Reid 1995). A quantitative prediction,

---

21.    It may appear there's a methodological problem in supporting the meaning hypothesis for *look* through appealing to the dictionary definition of another word for which there is no hypothesis. Note, however, that this analysis does not depend on a meaning hypothesis for *notice*; to support the hypothesis for *look* it is sufficient to appeal to the effect *notice* has on the communicated message – this effect is captured by the dictionary definition.

22.    Note that while *look* contributes to the message the notion of visual attention, VISUAL cannot by itself explain why *look* is the attested form in the example rather than, say, *see*, which by hypothesis also has VISUAL in its meaning. The presence of *notice* suggests a message feature of attention and thus offers support specifically for ATTENTION in the meaning of *look*.

then, is designed to establish the generality of the communicative strategy – the reason for using the form – proposed in the analysis of a particular example. Following the analysis of example (26), it is predicted that *look* and *notice* have a higher than chance frequency of co-occurring. In making this prediction, the predictive term *notice* functions as a surrogate for the suggestion of a message feature of attention; the confirmation of the prediction, that is, the greater than chance co-occurrence of the predictive term with *look*, affirms that this message feature – which is hypothesized to be part of the meaning – regularly motivates the choice to utter *look*.

Now, it would do no good to simply check the number of times *look* and *notice* co-occur in the corpus because an absolute number by itself cannot tell us whether the co-occurrence of two forms is to be considered higher than chance, that is, whether the two forms co-occur more frequently than the null hypothesis would predict. Rather, another form must be recruited to serve as a control against which the relative frequency of *look* and the predictive term can be compared. The only criterion for the control is that it will be a form whose contributions to the ongoing message are distinct from what is contributed by the meaning of *look*. Then, the prediction will be that *look* will co-occur with the predictive term more frequently than with the control term. The form *walk* will serve as the control term here because, while we do not have a full meaning hypothesis for *walk*, we know enough about it to assume that it is not chosen by speakers so as to suggest a message feature of attention (or of visual). Thus, when *walk* occurs in the same utterance as *look* then whatever reasons that may have led the speaker to utter *walk* are different from the reasons leading to the choice of *look*. Consider example (27).

(27)　[Describing a bikers' gathering:] You park your bike. You **walk** around. You **look** at the other bikes. You **look** at the women. You **look** at the concessions…                              (*NPR; Return of the Wild Ones*)

In this example, the speaker uses *walk* to suggest a message feature of movement by foot, whereas *look* is still chosen to suggest a message feature of visual attention. There is, therefore, no shared reason that motivates the speaker to utter these two forms together. Note that this does not preclude the two forms from co-occurring sometimes, as they do in (27); it is just that when they co-occur the speaker is choosing each form to produce different and non-overlapping message effects.

It is predicted, then, that *look* will favor *notice* in comparison to *walk*. This is how the prediction is tested. First, the total number of occurrences is collected for each of the following favored and disfavored sequences in COCA (Table 3).

**Table 3.** COCA searches for *notice* and *walk*

|            | Sequence                        | Tokens |
|------------|---------------------------------|--------|
| Favored    | *[notice]* [up to 5 slots] *[look]* | 554    |
| Disfavored | *[walk]* [up to 5 slots] *[look]*   | 692    |

The square brackets in the middle indicate that any sequence of a length that is between zero to five forms – including either words or punctuation marks – may intervene between the predictive/control term and *look*. The square brackets around the forms indicate that all possible forms of a word are counted in a single search (so, for example, *look*, *looks*, *looked* and *looking* are all counted together when searching for *[look]*). These searches indicate how many times *look* occurs in proximity (of up to 5 intervening forms/punctuation marks) to *notice* and to *walk*.

Of course, mere proximity cannot guarantee that *notice* and *look* both respond to the same aspect of the message. For instance, the search may yield a result such as *I told her that I never notice these things. She looked at me blankly...* In such an example, *notice* and *look* occur in close proximity and each form may well suggest a message feature of attention, but a qualitative analysis of this example probably could not appeal to *notice* to support ATTENTION in the meaning of *look*, because each form has probably been chosen in response to a different aspect of the communication. The problem is not that *notice* and *look* are in different sentences; the two forms appear in different sentences back in Example (26), too. In Example (26), however, both forms respond to the same aspect of the communication, that is, both respond to a message concerning Peter's attitude toward other people. But in the example given here the looking and the noticing are done by different people. Still, if there were no association between *look* and *notice*, that is, if any time these two forms co-occurred then each form were chosen for reasons completely independent of the other, then the results of the count ought to reveal no particular favoring of *look* toward *notice* in comparison to *walk*.

Finally, in addition to the searches described above, two more counts are required to test the prediction, that is, it is necessary to have the total number of occurrences of *notice* and the total number of occurrences of *walk*. These numbers provide a baseline for the relative frequency of *notice* to *walk* in the corpus, independent of *look*. Then, the relative frequency of *notice* to *walk* in the absence of *look* can be compared to the relative frequency of *notice* to *walk* in the presence of *look*. The prediction is that, in the presence of *look*, the frequency of *notice* relative to *walk* will be higher than the frequency of *notice* relative to *walk* in the absence of *look*. Table 4 presents the results for this count.

**Table 4.** Total COCA occurrences of *notice* and *walk* in the presence and absence of *look*

|  | *look* present | | *look* absent | |
|---|---|---|---|---|
|  | N | % | N | % |
| *notice* | 554 | 44 | 52943 | 27 |
| *walk* | 692 | 56 | 146791 | 73 |
| Total | 1246 | 100 | 199734 | 100 |
| $p < .0001$ | | | | |

The prediction is confirmed. The right column of Table 4 (titled '*look* absent') shows the baseline frequency of *notice* and *walk*; the left column (titled '*look* present') shows that the prediction is confirmed. The right side shows the number of all occurrences of *notice* and *walk* except those where these words occur with *look*. Under these baseline conditions, that is, with no *look* to impact its distribution, *notice* represents only 27 percent of the *notice-walk* total. The left side of the table shows the number of occurrences in the corpus of *notice* and *walk* in the presence of *look*. It turns out that *notice* now represents 44 percent of the *notice-walk* total. In other words, the presence of *look* is associated with an increase of 17 percentage points (i.e., from 27 percent to 44 percent) in the frequency of *notice* compared to *walk* from the baseline rate. The very low *p* value shows that these results are highly statistically significant.[23]

Since the quantitative prediction was testing for the generality of the communicative strategy proposed in the analysis of Example (26), its confirmation in Table 4 argues that the proposed communicative strategy – the reason motivating speakers to choose both *look* and *notice* – is quite regularly deployed. Note that the meaning hypothesis itself has not been directly tested, and so has not been directly supported by the counts, either. Rather, the meaning hypothesis is indirectly supported through the testing of the generality of the communicative strategy which, in turn, follows from the meaning hypothesis. In this case, the communicative strategy to suggest a message feature of attention follows from the meaning hypothesis ATTENTION, VISUAL and so, indirectly supports it.

## 2.2    Justification of the inductive approach

The reader may wonder why the analysis of a particular example was necessary; why not make quantitative predictions directly on the basis of the meaning hypothesis for *look* and the posited meaning of the predictive term, such as *notice*?

---

23.    But see footnote 14 (in Chapter 1, Section 3.2).

Such a proposal would entail that a quantitative prediction can be derived deductively from the meanings themselves – that is, from a consideration of the meanings abstracted from particular occasions of their use.[24] The reasons for rejecting this deductive approach are discussed presently.

If a quantitative prediction were derived deductively directly from the meanings of the forms in question, the rationale for the predicted favoring would have to be stated in terms of the compatibility of the meanings themselves. In the case at hand, the rationale would be that *look* and *notice* are expected to co-occur relatively frequently because their meanings are compatible. It may be that the meanings of both *look* and *notice* have ATTENTION in them; but, as we shall see in this and the next chapter, there are some predictive terms (e.g., *at* or *but*) whose meanings have no semantic substance in common with *look* and yet an overlap in the reason for the choice of each form is still evident. But even for cases where the two meanings do share some semantic substance, the essential problem is that meanings are not independently attracted to one another simply by virtue of their compatibility; rather, there is a person who must choose to utter certain forms together as opposed to others. A purely deductive explanation – one which appeals to the meanings alone but not to speakers' choices – would take the human out of the explanation. The express goal of the meaning hypothesis, however, is precisely to explain human speaking and writing behavior in terms of expressive choices. A rationale in terms of a communicative strategy is therefore preferred as it is based on a speaker's expressive choice demonstrated in a particular case, and tests for the generality of that principle of choice.

Now a communicative strategy cannot be appealed to in the absence of an initial demonstration through a particular example because, without an example there is simply no evidence that the purported communicative strategy actually exists. It is true that, as speakers of the language, even without seeing a particular example, we may imagine that people would choose to use *look* and *notice* in the same utterance; but this would make the account dependent on our intuitions as speakers; that is, the quantitative count would then test our intuitions rather than testing speakers' expressive choices. Thus, strict methodology requires first a demonstration that a certain communicative strategy – such as where *look* and *notice* are both chosen to suggest a message feature of attention – has indeed motivated a speaker, at least once (see also Diver 1995: 110). The quantitative prediction then tests the extent to which this communicative strategy is representative of other tokens in the corpus at large.

---

24. This type of deductive rationale for quantitative predictions has been suggested in Diver (1969) as discussed at length in Reid (1995) and in Davis (2004).

To sum up the methodological procedure, each subsection within Sections 3 and 4 below will begin with a qualitative analysis of a particular example demonstrating that a speaker's choice to utter *look* plausibly follows from the hypothesized meaning ATTENTION, VISUAL. Each such demonstration will point to the presence of a certain other form whose contribution to the message partially overlaps with the contribution made by *look* – if the hypothesized meaning of *look* is correct. Section 3 will focus on forms suggestive of attention, while Section 4 will focus on forms suggestive of visual. Taking then these predictive forms as surrogates for the message effect – of attention, in Section 3, and of visual, in Section 4 – each quantitative prediction will test the generality of the communicative strategy proposed in the analysis of the relevant example.

## 3.   Supporting ATTENTION in the meaning of *look*

This section points to six different predictive terms that can serve as surrogates for the suggestion of a message feature of attention, and thereby support ATTENTION in the hypothesized meaning of *look*. These forms are: *carefully, this, but, at, deliberately* and *think*. While these patterns (that is, *look carefully, look at this,* etc.) all support ATTENTION in the meaning of *look*, it is worthwhile to go through the demonstration with each one of them, not only because each strengthens the meaning hypothesis but also because each furthers the goal of accounting for the asymmetries observed in the corpus with respect to *look*.

One final preliminary note is in order. In some of the subsections below, qualitative analyses are offered for both an example featuring the predictive term as well as an example featuring the control term; for instance, Section 3.1 analyzes an example of *look carefully* and then also an example of *look carelessly*. In other subsections, however, a qualitative analysis is offered only for an example featuring the predictive term; for instance, Section 3.2 analyzes an example of *look at this* but not an example of *look at the* (*the* is the control term). The reason for this discrepancy in the presentation is that some control terms – such as *carelessly* – seem to suggest message features that may appear inherently at odds with the message feature of attention suggested by *look*, and so, it is of special interest to demonstrate to skeptical readers how it is that the two forms do, nonetheless, sometimes co-occur. Other control terms – such as *the* – suggest message features that, while having no overlap with the notion of visual attention suggested by *look*, are simply neutral to it, and so, there is no reason for any reader to suppose that these control terms and *look* should not co-occur sometimes.

### 3.1 Using *carefully* to support ATTENTION

(28)   "We have had intelligence reports that Germany is developing a very large missile. I ordered photo reconnaissance of the Baltic Coast, where the test flights were taking place. These photographs are the result." He handed me an envelope. The photographs were dated the twelfth and twenty third of June, 1943, and upon both were circles drawn in black ink. I **looked carefully** at the blurred but sleek images within the circles. "These are indeed rockets," I said. "How big are they?" "About forty feet long, and they are sitting on thirty-ton trailers." *(Ninety Thousand Horses)*

To begin with the qualitative analysis, in this text, the author chose *look* because the message involves the speaker having directed visual attention to the image in the photo and, by hypothesis, ATTENTION, VISUAL is the meaning of *look*. Various contextual features indicate that visual attention is here at issue. First, the object of attention is the image in a photo, thus supporting VISUAL. Second, the image is *blurred*, and yet, despite its blurriness, the speaker still perceives rockets, even indicating their size and precisely what they are sitting on; the perception of such details thus supports ATTENTION. Third, the use of *carefully* suggests that the act is performed with some degree of concentration and care, again supporting ATTENTION.

Turning to the quantitative test, in regard to the third point, note that the writer's reason for choosing *carefully* partially intersects with the reason for choosing *look* (as opposed to, say, *see*). *Carefully*, therefore, may function as a surrogate for a message feature of attention in order to test the claim that speakers regularly choose *look* in light of the suggestion of a message feature of attention. The form *carelessly*, which suggests lack of attention, will serve as the control term against which the predicted favoring of *look* to *carefully* can be tested. It is predicted, then, that *look* will favor *carefully* in comparison to *carelessly* because *look* and *carefully* may be chosen by speakers to produce a similar effect on the message whereas *look* and *carelessly* are not.

To test this prediction the following searches in COCA are carried out (Table 5).

**Table 5.** COCA searches for *carefully* and *carelessly*

|  | Sequence | Tokens |
|---|---|---|
| Favored | *[look] carefully*<br>*carefully [look]* | 485 |
| Disfavored | *[look] carelessly*<br>*carelessly [look]* | 0 |

In addition, two more counts were made, one for the total number of occurrences of *carefully* and another for the total number of occurrences of *carelessly*. Table 6 presents the results of the prediction.

**Table 6.**  Total COCA occurrences of *carefully* and *carelessly* in the presence and absence of *look*

|  | *look* present | | *look* absent | |
| --- | --- | --- | --- | --- |
|  | N | % | N | % |
| *carefully* | 485 | 100 | 25220 | 97.5 |
| *carelessly* | 0 | 0 | 638 | 2.5 |
| Total | 485 | 100 | 25917 | 100 |
| p < .001 | | | | |

The prediction is confirmed. Again, the right column shows the baseline distribution; the left column shows the prediction. In the right column we see that *carefully* comprises 97.5 percent of the *carefully-carelessly* total. The left column then shows the forms' relative distribution once *look* is introduced as the immediately preceding or immediately following word, showing an increase from 97.5 to 100 percent in the context of *look*, indicating that *look* favors *carefully* in comparison to *carelessly*. It is true that the percentage skewing is not much, only 2.5 percentage points, yet as indicated by the *p* value the probability of this favoring being due to chance is quite low. This data confirms the generality of the communicative strategy proposed in the analysis of Example (28). In making the quantitative prediction, the predictive term *carefully* functions as a surrogate for the suggestion of a message feature of attention. Its relatively frequent co-occurrence with *look*, therefore, indirectly supports the meaning hypothesis because, following the hypothesis, *look* is also (partially) chosen for a similar message feature of attention.

Two further points are in order concerning the above data, having to do with the low numbers for *carelessly* and the complete absence of *look-carelessly* combinations in COCA. First, *carelessly* occurs in the corpus at large merely 638 times. Yet it does not follow from this low number that *carelessly* will be disfavored in the context of just any form as it is disfavored in the context of *look*. Thus, in the context of the word *say*, for instance, *carelessly* is in fact the favored form.[25]

---

**25.**  A quantitative test run on background reveals that in the context of what is perhaps the most generic activity – *do* – neither *carefully* nor *carelessly* are favored; that is, neither form occurs more frequently than the null hypothesis would predict in the presence of *do* compared to the absence of *do*. This fact further strengthens the claim that the favoring of *look* toward *carefully* is indeed unique to *look* and follows from its hypothesized meaning.

As Table 7 indicates, in direct opposition to the skewing observed with *look*, in the context of *say* it is the percentage of *carelessly* that rises, from 2.5 to 5 percent.[26]

**Table 7.** Total COCA occurrences of *carefully* and *carelessly* in the presence and absence of *say*

|  | *say* present | | *say* absent | |
|---|---|---|---|---|
|  | N | % | N | % |
| *carelessly* | 12 | 5 | 626 | 2.5 |
| *carefully* | 215 | 95 | 25490 | 97.5 |
| Total | 216 | 100 | 26116 | 100 |
| p < .01 | | | | |

Coming now to the second point, while not a single occurrence of *look carelessly* is found in COCA, this does not mean that such a sequence is ungrammatical or communicatively incoherent. It may seem that such a sequence ought to be incoherent, for if *look* suggests the notion of attention, and *carelessly* the lack of attention then, their being used together should seem inherently incompatible. But contexts do arise in which *look carelessly* is precisely what the speaker or writer wants to communicate, as in (29).

(29)   A pleasant method of giving a child a lesson in attention may be found in Ogden's "Science of Education". He says: "A little expedient to which I have resorted, on some occasions, may be suggestive of means that may be adopted for correcting these evils, and of fixing the attention. Holding up my watch to the school, I have said: 'How many of these little boys and girls can **look** at it for one minute at a time?' The idea, perhaps, is a novel one, and their little voices and hands will respond, anxious for the experiment. Some will say, boastingly, 'I can **look** at it an hour!', '*two hours!*' responds

---

**26.**   Another reason this supplemental comparison of *look* to *say* is worthwhile is in light of Vendler's (1957) distinction between activity verbs and state verbs. According to Vendler, one of the tests for distinguishing between these two types of verbs is whether the word *carefully* can modify it; if *carefully* is a proper modification then it must be an activity verb. Thus, one might argue that *carefully* is expected to co-occur with *look* simply because *look* is an activity verb, not necessarily because of the suggestion of attention in particular. But at least some activities can be performed either carefully or carelessly, that is, either with or without concentration of attention. The fact that *look* favors *carefully* in comparison to *carelessly* is a specific consequence of the hypothesized meaning of *look*, and cannot be attributed simply to a classification of *look* as an activity verb; indeed, other activity verbs, such as *say*, may (and in the case of *say*, do) favor *carelessly* in comparison to *carefully*.

another little captain, who is anxious to make a display of his prowess. At this juncture, I ask, how many would be willing to make the experiment of one minute continuous **looking**? There is a shower of hands and a shout of voices raised to the highest pitch. 'Well, let us try; all ready; now!' And their forms straighten up, and all eyes are bent with intense earnestness upon the watch. It grows very quiet, and everyone listens and **looks**. Presently it occurs to half a dozen, or more, of them, that they are doing it about right. 'I wonder if John, or Charles, or Mary, or Ellen, is **looking** too? Wonder if they all are doing as well I am?' And their thoughts leave the watch and the promise, and wander after Charles, or Ellen, and the temptation to **look** away becomes so great that in about half a minute, or less, you will see an occasional pair of eyes glance hurriedly to some convenient corner of the room, and back quick to the watch again; others, still less cautious, will turn the head, and **look carelessly** away; others, again, will drop off entirely, and cease to **look**, while some, more resolute and determined and careful than the rest, will not remove their eyes for a moment, and at the expiration of the time, will announce their triumph with evident satisfaction.

> (*Proceedings of the California State Teachers' Institute and Educational Convention*)

*Look* is used many times throughout this text because the topic of the text concerns teaching children attention.[27] Evidence in support of the hypothesis is provided in sequences such as *fixing the attention, their forms straighten up* and *all eyes are bent with intense earnestness*. Now, we all know how difficult it can be to sustain attention for extended periods of time without interruption. Other stimuli, whether visual or not, may catch hold of one's attention, causing one to involuntarily divert their eyes without intending to do so (Hatfield 1998). The use of both *carelessly* and *less cautious* suggest that some children involuntarily shift their attention away from the watch without intention or notice.

What is important is that the writer's choice of *carelessly* and the choice of *look* are each made in light of different, non-overlapping, message effects. *Look* produces a message feature of visual attention, as is well supported throughout the text, while *carelessly* contributes to a message feature of momentary mindlessness, indeed, the opposite of attention. Example (29) thus demonstrates how it is that *look* and *carelessly* can sometimes co-occur, and also explains why the two forms are expected to co-occur less frequently in comparison to *look* with *carefully*.

---

**27.** Note that *look* accounts for 2.3 percent of the words in this text whereas in COCA at large *look* accounts for merely 0.1 percent. This prominence of *look* in a text whose entire theme is visual attention in and of itself provides strong support for the meaning hypothesis.

## 3.2   Using *this* to support ATTENTION

(30)   [Dominique and Peter are discussing their dinner plans:] "We have the
Palmers for dinner tomorrow night," she said. "Oh, Christ!" he moaned.
"They're such awful bores! Why do we have to have them?" She stood
holding the calendar forward between the tips of her fingers, as if she were a
photograph with the focus on the calendar and her own figure blurred in its
background. [...] "Would you like to **look** at **this** calendar, Peter?"

(*The Fountainhead*)

Beginning again with the qualitative analysis, in this example, the author chose
*look* because Dominique is trying to direct Peter's attention to the calendar she is
holding. Contextual evidence is provided in the sequence *as if she were a photograph with the focus on the calendar and her own figure blurred in its background*;
the use of *photograph* and *blurred* clearly support VISUAL, and the use of both *focus
on the calendar* and *her own figure is blurred in its background* support ATTENTION.
Yet further support for the hypothesis comes from the use of *this* in the sequence
*look at this*. To understand the author's choice of *this*, a brief explanation concerning this form's meaning hypothesis is necessary.

Following Diver (2012), the forms *this* and *that* (as well as *these* and *those*) are
hypothesized to constitute a grammatical system that signals information concerning what Diver called Deixis, that is, degree of attention. The meaning of *this*, by
hypothesis is MORE DEIXIS, and of *that* LESS DEIXIS. In our example, *this* is used in
response to the attention-worthiness or emphasis given by the speaker to the entity
at hand (the calendar). Indeed, the choice of *this* in (30) contributes to the high
degree of prominence given to the calendar, as evidenced also by the sequence *focus
on the calendar* mentioned above. Similarly, the choice of *look* is, by hypothesis,
partially made in response to the same notional fragment of the message, that is,
the prominence or attention-worthiness of the calendar in the scene. It is therefore predicted that *look* will co-occur with *this* at a higher than chance frequency
because both forms are chosen to produce a message feature of attention.

As before, a control term must be recruited. It may appear that *this* should be
compared to *that*. Such a comparison, however, is not useful here because *that*,
like *this*, is also a member of the system of Deixis; though the hypothesized meaning of *that* is LESS DEIXIS, still, speakers utter *that* to produce a message feature of
increased attention, too. The communicative strategy rationale cannot, therefore,
distinguish between *this* and *that* because both of these forms, much like *look*, are
chosen to suggest a notion of attention. In order to test the favoring of *look* to *this*
we need a control term whose choice has nothing to do with the suggestion of
attention (and of visual, too). The form *the* fits the bill. Without going into unnecessary detail, the hypothesized meaning of *the* is DIFFERENTIATION REQUIRED AND

COMPLETE (Reid 1991: 79). This meaning instructs the addressee that a discrete entity is at issue (differentiation required) and that the addressee has sufficient information to identify which entity it is (complete). What is important is that the meaning of *the* has nothing to do with the suggestion of a notion of visual attention, and so, when it co-occurs with *look*, the reasons for its deployment are completely different from the speaker's reasons for choosing *look*.

To test this prediction the following searches in COCA are carried out (Table 8).

**Table 8.** COCA searches for *this* and *the*

|  | Sequence | Tokens |
|---|---|---|
| Favored | [look] at this | 7953 |
|  | look, this |  |
| Disfavored | [look] at the | 44798 |
|  | look, the |  |

The search is sensitive to punctuation so that, regarding the second sequence in each row, only occurrences where there is a comma between *look* and the predictive/control term are counted. Note that many of the occurrences of *look, this* and *look, the* are cases where conceptual metaphor is involved, as for example in *Look, this is what I'm trying to say* or *look, the idea is simple*. The confirmation of the prediction thus argues that the hypothesized meaning ATTENTION, VISUAL is applicable to both the visual and intellectual uses. Table 9 presents the results of this prediction.

**Table 9.** Total COCA occurrences of *this* and *the* in the presence and absence of *look*

|  | *look* present | | *look* absent | |
|---|---|---|---|---|
|  | N | % | N | % |
| *this* | 7953 | 15 | 2169579 | 8 |
| *the* | 44798 | 85 | 25019156 | 92 |
| Total | 52751 | 100 | 27188735 | 100 |
| p < .0001 | | | | |

The right column shows that, in the absence of *look*, *this* constitutes 8 percent of the *this-the* total. Once *look* is introduced, however, *this* skews in the predicted direction, accounting now for 15 percent of the total. The *p* value indicates that the probability of the association between *look* and *this* being due to chance is extremely low. This data, therefore, confirms the generality of the communicative strategy that speakers deploy *look* to suggest a message feature of attention, and so indirectly supports the hypothesized meaning of *look*.

We take here the opportunity to note that this favoring is unique to *look* and that other forms from the visual domain, such as *glance* (Tables 10 and 11) and *stare* (Tables 12 and 13), do not show any such favoring toward *this*.[28]

**Table 10.** COCA searches for *this* and *the* (for *glance*)

| [glance] at this | [glance] at the |
|---|---|

**Table 11.** Total COCA occurrences of *this* and *the* in the presence and absence of *glance*

|  | *glance* present | | *glance* absent | |
|---|---|---|---|---|
|  | N | % | N | % |
| *the* | 3139 | 99 | 25060815 | 92 |
| *this* | 27 | 1 | 2177505 | 8 |
| Total | 3166 | 100 | 8002352 | 100 |
| p < .0001 | | | | |

**Table 12.** COCA searches for *this* and *the* (for *stare*)

| [stare] at this | [stare] at the |
|---|---|

**Table 13.** Total COCA occurrences of *this* and *the* in the presence and absence of *stare*

|  | *stare* present | | *stare* absent | |
|---|---|---|---|---|
|  | N | % | N | % |
| *the* | 7235 | 98 | 25056719 | 92 |
| *this* | 112 | 2 | 2177420 | 8 |
| Total | 7347 | 100 | 8002352 | 100 |
| p < .0001 | | | | |

For reasons currently unknown, in the presence of both *glance* and *stare* – unlike in the presence of *look* – it is the frequency of *the* in comparison to *this* that increases, by seven and six percentage points respectively.[29]

---

28. A detailed analysis comparing the distribution of *look* to that of *see* is offered in Chapter 4.

29. It is interesting that *glance* and *stare* favor *the* in comparison to *this*, but it is outside the scope of this research to explain this tendency. A thorough analysis of the forms *glance* and *stare* would be required.

## 3.3    Using *but* to support ATTENTION

(31)    [Peter Keating, a relatively new employee, offers to do a favor to his col-
league, Davis, to complete Davis's drawings:] "Wait," said Keating, and
leaned closer to him. "Wait! There's another way. I'll finish them for you."
"Huh?" "I'll stay. I'll do them. Don't be afraid. No one'll tell the difference."
"Pete! Would you?" "Sure. I've nothing to do tonight. You just stay till they
all go home, then skip." "Oh, gee, Pete!" Davis sighed, tempted. "**But look**,
if they find out, they'll can me. You're too new for this kind of job." "They
won't find out." "I can't lose my job, Pete. You know I can't. Elaine and I are
going to be married soon. If anything happens…" "Nothing will happen."
*(The Fountainhead)*

In regard to this example, we will now argue that the use of *but* provides contextual evidence in support of ATTENTION in the meaning of *look*. To understand
the argument, a brief explanation of the semantic contribution of *but* is in order.
According to Crupi (2004), the form *but* is used so as to override some aspect in
the discourse that precedes it; Crupi calls this the override-effect of *but*. In this
example, Davis is using *but* so as to override his initial expression of excitement
(*Oh, gee, Pete!*) in order to clear the way for expressing his grave concerns (*if they
find out, they'll can me*). Crupi goes on to demonstrate that by overriding what
comes before *but*, the use of *but* simultaneously suggests the thematic importance
of what follows it. In this text, the thematic importance of the information following *but* is evident in the sequences *I can't lose my job* and *you know I can't*, suggesting the high stakes at issue.

Now, the choice to utter *look* contributes to a similar message effect as is
achieved by uttering *but*; that is, Davis is choosing *look* so as to further strengthen
the thematic importance of the following information by expressly calling for
Peter's attention before presenting it. Thus, *but* and *look* function harmoniously to
yield one message effect, both suggesting that what is coming up is quite important.

It is worth pointing out that a deductive rationale could not predict that *look*
would regularly co-occur with *but* because the meanings of these two signs share
no common semantic substance and thus do not overlap semantically. Rather, it
is the communicative strategy of when to use *but* that overlaps with that of *look*.
As evidenced in the analysis of Example 31, both words are sometimes used to
produce the same effect in the message even though the two words have nothing
semantically in common (see also Reid 1991: 304).

To make a prediction concerning the regular co-occurrence of *but* and *look*,
the form *and* is recruited as a control term. *And*, like *but*, serves as a link between
two pieces of information, yet unlike *but*, *and* is used merely to signal an additive
connection, and has nothing to do with suggesting the thematic importance of, or
calling attention to, information that follows it (Crupi 2004). The prediction then

is that *look* will favor *but* in comparison to *and*. The following COCA searches are carried out (Table 14), followed by the results (Table 15).

**Table 14.**  COCA searches for *but* and *and*

|            | Sequence   | Tokens |
|------------|------------|--------|
| Favored    | *but look* | 2136   |
|            | *but, look* |       |
| Disfavored | *and look* | 8569   |
|            | *and, look* |       |

**Table 15.**  Total COCA occurrences of *but* and *and* in the presence and absence of *look*

|       | *look* present | | *look* absent | |
|-------|------|-----|----------|-----|
|       | N    | %   | N        | %   |
| *but* | 2136 | 20  | 2079131  | 14  |
| *and* | 8569 | 80  | 12343025 | 86  |
| Total | 10705 | 100 | 14422156 | 100 |
| p < .0001 | | | | |

The right column shows that in the absence of *look*, *but* accounts for 14 percent of the *but-and* total. In the presence of *look*, however, it accounts for 20 percent. As indicated by the *p* value, the probability of this association being due to chance is quite low. This quantitative data shows that Example (31) is only a part of a more general pattern of the distribution of *look* and *but*. Again, the same rationale that explains the individual example also explains the quantitative favoring throughout a large corpus.

Note lastly that though Example (31) appears not to involve any element of visual in the message, the choice to utter *look* still follows from the meaning ATTENTION, VISUAL due to the cognitive metaphor mapping vision to intellection, as has been discussed in Chapter 2 (in this example, Peter is asked to direct his intellectual attention to Davis's concerns). As was noted in regard to Tables 8 and 9 above (*look, this/the*), here too, the confirmation of the prediction argues that the hypothesized meaning is applicable to both the visual and intellectual uses.

## 3.4    Using *at* to support ATTENTION

(32)    [Yoga instructor:] The tree is a balancing posture. Now the trick to doing balancing postures is to find one spot of attention on the floor or, in front of you on the wall, and this gives you concentration, by **looking at** one spot.

> [...] We're going to start by moving your weight over to your right foot, and bringing your left foot either to your ankle, calf or to the inside of your thigh, taking your time, finding your position, bringing your hands into a prayer position in front of your chest, **looking at** one spot of attention either in front of you or on the floor...
>
> (*MBSR YOGA #2 – https://www.youtube.com/watch?v=PElmyy_kwN0*)

The meaning of *look* is chosen because the message involves an instruction to visually attend to one spot. Note the contextual evidence supporting the hypothesized meaning of *look*. First, balancing oneself requires concentration and attention, and the word *attention* straightforwardly figures in the text twice, clearly supporting ATTENTION. Next, the use of *spot* also supports ATTENTION as it indicates a visual stimulus that is as narrow as can be; recall, in this respect, the discussion in Chapter 2 concerning the experiential association between visual attention and narrowing of the visual field ("the greater the attention, the smaller the part of the visual field to which it extends", Hatfield 1998). Lastly, the use of *at* further contributes to a similar message feature of focus and attention.

To understand this contribution by *at*, a brief explanation of its hypothesized meaning is in order. The form *at*, along with *on* and *in*, constitute a system of signs signaling information concerning the number of dimensions conceptualized for a location (Reid 2004); *at* signals the meaning ZERO DIMENSIONAL LOCATION (that is, a point-like location), *in* signals THREE DIMENSIONAL LOCATION and *on* signals OTHER THAN ZERO AND THREE DIMENSIONAL LOCATION.

Thus, much like the use of *spot*, the meaning of *at* contributes to a message feature of focus and attention because it suggests, in this context, a narrowing of the visual field up to just a single point. And *look*, by hypothesis, also suggests a narrowing of the visual field because visual attention involves selecting and focusing one's eyes to a particular visual stimulus at the expense of its surroundings. Indeed, attention inherently involves shutting things out, seeing as one's attention cannot be everywhere at once. In Example (32), the instructor suggests with the use of *look* and of *at* that all visual stimuli are to be shut out except for the narrow point where one's visual attention is focused.

Because the meanings of both *look* and *at* may contribute to a similar message effect of attention, it is predicted that *look* will co-occur with *at* at a higher than chance frequency. This prediction will be tested through a comparison to *on* and *in*, serving as the control terms. *On* and *in*, due to their hypothesized meanings, cannot contribute to a message concerning the narrowing of the visual field because the spatial location their meanings suggest is broader than a mere point. Thus, when these forms occur following *look*, the reason for their deployment has nothing to do with the notions of focus or attention, and so, *look* is not expected to show any particular favoring toward these forms.

The following searches in COCA are carried out (Table 16).

**Table 16.** COCA searches for *at, on* and *in*

|            | Sequence   | Tokens |
|------------|------------|--------|
| Favored    | *[look] at*  | 176841 |
| Disfavored | *[look] on*  | 5353   |
|            | *[look] in*  | 8170   |

**Table 17.** Total COCA occurrences of *at, on* and *in* in the presence and absence of *look*

|       | *look* present | | *look* absent | |
|-------|------|------|------|------|
|       | N | % | N | % |
| *at*    | 176841 | 93  | 2089402  | 15  |
| *on*    | 5353   | 3   | 3129481  | 23  |
| *in*    | 8170   | 4   | 8355017  | 62  |
| Total   | 190364 | 100 | 13573900 | 100 |

$p < .0001$

The prediction is confirmed. The right column of Table 17 shows that when neutralizing the effect of *look*, *at* accounts for merely 15 percent of the *at-on-in* total. The left column shows that in the context of *look* the relative frequency of *at* rises to 93 percent of that total.

The results of this prediction are probably not too surprising (we all probably already knew that *look at* is most frequent). Yet it is important to appreciate that the prediction follows from the meaning hypotheses for the forms *look, at, on* and *in*. In the absence of a meaning hypothesis, the relatively frequent co-occurrence of *look* and *at* could seem purely arbitrary. It is also worthwhile to note that the sequences *look on* and *look in*, though they occur less frequently, nonetheless do occur. Indeed, there is nothing ungrammatical or semantically incoherent about putting these two forms together. Still, the reason these occur relatively infrequently is because each expressive choice – of *look* on the one hand and of either *on* or *in* on the other – is made in light of different communicative goals. This can be briefly demonstrated by means of the following example.

(33)   Mr. Gupton was the last man to stir the stew before they served it up, and he had been carrying his teeth in his shirt pocket to rest his gums. Well, everybody had commenced eating their portion except Mr. Gupton, and Milo noticed him frowning hard and feeling his pockets and **looking on** the ground all round the pot, so Milo went over and asked him was anything wrong, and he said, "I have mislaid my teeth."

(*A Long and Happy Life*)

In this example, the writer's motivation for choosing *on* is clearly not to suggest a message feature involving a point-like location, but rather a surface (*the ground all round the pot*). While the choice of *on* has nothing to do with the notion of narrowing the visual field, the author's choice of *look* is still motivated by the suggestion of a message feature of visual attention; the message involves Mr. Gupton thoroughly scanning the floor with attentive eyes.

## 3.5 Using *deliberately* to support ATTENTION

(34)  [Once the baby begins crawling…] The baby […] is no longer restricted by the entertaining items within arm's reach. Now he can go after what he wants without crying for help. Climbing is often another pleasure newly discovered at this stage. Malek says that crawling and creeping babies will **deliberately look** for small items to climb over in their path.
(*Today's parent – magazine; From Birth to One: Mobility*)

The writer here chose *look* because the message involves babies visually attending to objects in their path; note the babies have to visually examine the objects around them in order to make a climbing decision. Support for the hypothesis is evident in the use of *deliberately*, suggesting that the act is done through the use of conscious thought and willful, intentional direction of attention.

Because *look* and *deliberately* may both be chosen to produce a message feature of attention, the two forms are expected to co-occur at a higher than chance frequency. As usual, a comparison to a control term is required, and to this end the form *accidentally*, which suggests that an act is performed inattentively and unintentionally, is recruited. It is predicted, then, that *look* will favor *deliberately* in comparison to *accidentally*. The COCA searches for this prediction are the following (Table 18).

**Table 18.** COCA searches for *deliberately* and *accidentally*

|  | Sequence | Tokens |
|---|---|---|
| Favored | *deliberately [look]* | 21 |
| Disfavored | *accidentally [look]* | 2 |

**Table 19.** Total COCA occurrences of *deliberately* and *accidentally* in the presence and absence of *look*

|  | *look* present | | *look* absent | |
|---|---|---|---|---|
|  | N | % | N | % |
| *deliberately* | 21 | 91 | 5950 | 66 |
| *accidentally* | 2 | 9 | 3130 | 34 |
| Total | 23 | 100 | 9080 | 100 |

$p < .01$

The prediction is confirmed. The right column shows that in the neutralized condition, that is, in the absence of any potential effect of *look*, *deliberately* accounts for 66 percent of the *deliberately-accidentally* total. In the context of *look*, however, *deliberately* is clearly favored, constituting now 91 percent of the total. This data confirms the generality of the communicative strategy to utter both *look* and *deliberately* to produce a message feature of attention.

Now, it might appear that *accidentally* should never co-occur with *look* because it implies no deliberation and so seems to contradict the notion of attention suggested by the hypothesized meaning of *look*. But there is no contradiction. As noted, while humans do have a strong degree of control over where they direct their visual attention, it is not absolute, and involuntary shifts of attention may occur; we have already seen evidence of this in Example (29) above, where some of the children *carelessly* directed their attention away from the teacher's watch. Consider now Example (35) featuring *accidentally*.

(35)    [In the course of rock climbing…] [He] tightened his grip and moved
        up to the next knot, and then the next. He was doing it by feel now,
        because his eyes stung so badly from the sweat. Maybe it was a good thing
        he couldn't see, he told himself – then it wouldn't matter if he **accidentally
        looked** down.                                                      (*Rope*)

While it is true that the act of looking in this example is performed without intention or deliberation, the hypothesized meaning of *look* is still supported. The choice of *look* is here made in order to suggest the direction that the climber's eyes might follow, namely *down*. Indeed, the meaning ATTENTION, VISUAL can be used to contribute to a message concerning the direction that the eyes take because in an act of visual attention one naturally orients one's eyes toward the direction of attention. Now, as for *accidentally*, the climber is worried about the prospect of his eyes facing downward, because that would be quite frightening; still, his eyes might go facing downward without his intending to do so. The choice in *accidentally* suggests that the direction of the eyes downward might happen without intention, deliberation or conscious thought. What is important here is that each expressive choice – that of *look* on the one hand and of *accidentally* on the other – is made in light of different and non-overlapping communicative effects.

### 3.6    Using *think* to support ATTENTION

(36)    [Learning from the mistakes of the past in gardening:] Other plants had to
        be discarded either because their habit of growth offended me or they were
        ill placed. A whole group of Prunus subhirtella' Pendula' on the riverside
        lawn had to go; […] Six Swedish birches at the end of the south lawn also
        had to go (one good specimen still remains), for a glade of birches was not

> the answer there. My mistakes have taught me a lesson: **Look and think**
> **very hard before you leap!** (*Horticulture magazine*)

In this example, the writer chose *look* to express that, in the future, he must visually (and intellectually) attend to his garden to allow him to better plan his actions. Support for the hypothesis comes from the use of *think*, suggesting that the writer must devote some conscious mental effort to considering his actions. When one is actively directing their thoughts toward something, then one is at the same time giving attention to that object of thought; indeed, our running thoughts are indicative of where our (intellectual/mental) attention is at a given moment. It may lastly be noted that both *look* and *think* are together modified by *very hard*, suggesting that both the attending and the considering will be performed rigorously, further supporting ATTENTION.

Following this example, it is predicted that *look* and *think* will co-occur at a higher than chance frequency because, through its suggestion of directed mental activity, *think* contributes to a message feature of attention, as, by hypothesis, *look* does too. For this prediction, the form *believe* will serve as the control term. While we do not know what precisely is the semantic contribution of *believe*, it is safe to assume that *believe* does not indicate mental activity but a rather passive mental state or disposition. Thus, when *look* and *believe* co-occur then each form produces different and non-overlapping effects in the message.

The COCA searches are the following (Table 20).

**Table 20.** COCA searches for *think* and *believe*

|  | Sequence | Tokens |
|---|---|---|
| Favored | *look* [up to 3 slots] *and think* | 472 |
| Disfavored | *look* [up to 3 slots] *and believe* | 21 |

**Table 21.** Total COCA occurrences of *think* and *believe* in the presence and absence of *look*

|  | *look* present | | *look* absent | |
|---|---|---|---|---|
|  | N | % | N | % |
| *think* | 472 | 96 | 889446 | 82 |
| *believe* | 21 | 4 | 201765 | 18 |
| Total | 493 | 100 | 1091211 | 100 |
| $p < .0001$ | | | | |

The prediction is confirmed. The right column of Table 21 shows that, in the absence of *look*, *think* accounts for 82 percent of the *think-believe* total. In the context of *look*, however, there is a clear favoring toward *think*, as in the left column it rises to 96 percent of the total.

An objection may be raised as to the interpretation of the results of this prediction. Vendler (1957) distinguishes between activity verbs and state verbs. This distinction is relevant here because, whereas *believe* is classified as a state verb, Vendler observes that *think* is ambiguous. Thus, Vendler argues, in a sentence such as *I am thinking about John*, then *think* indeed denotes a mental activity and so – I say – suggests that the speaker is directing attention to John; but in a sentence such as *I think John is nice*, then here, argues Vendler, *think* denotes merely a mental state, without necessarily implying that the speaker is actively attending their thoughts toward John.

Of course, these examples are made up by the analyst and further, a meaning hypothesis for *think* is currently not available. Still, it is acknowledged that there may be a problem here. Thus, while it is clear in Example (36) that *think* suggests a message of mental activity, one cannot be certain that *think* suggests such mental activity in all the other 471 occurrences in COCA where *think* coincides with *look*. This is important because the entire basis for the rationale of this prediction rests on the assumption that *think* contributes to a message feature of mental activity.

There is a way, however, to handle this difficulty even in the absence of a full-fledged meaning hypothesis for *think*. Vendler proposes that the presence of -*ing* is indicative of an activity use of *think*. Observe, then, that the prediction that *look* favors *think* in comparison to *believe* is confirmed even when counting only the cases of *thinking* and *believing* (Table 22).

As is evident, the results in Table 22 are quite similar to the results in Table 21.

**Table 22.** Total COCA occurrences of *thinking* and *believing* in the presence and absence of *look*

|  | *look* present | | *look* absent | |
| --- | --- | --- | --- | --- |
|  | N | % | N | % |
| *thinking* | 88 | 97 | 889830 | 82 |
| *believing* | 3 | 3 | 201783 | 18 |
| Total | 91 | 100 | 1091613 | 100 |
| p < .0005 | | | | |

## 4.   Supporting VISUAL in the meaning of *look*

This section offers quantitative predictions that support VISUAL in the meaning of *look*. Though it may seem straightforward that VISUAL figures in the meaning of *look*, still, in light of theories that analyze *look* in terms of polysemy, it is important to demonstrate that the inclusion of VISUAL in the hypothesized meaning of *look* is statistically supported. While *look* is used both for visual and intellectual messages, the counts below reveal that visual messages are highly statistically favored, thus supporting the inclusion of VISUAL in the meaning hypothesis.

Each of the three subsections below presents an example featuring a form other than *look* that suggests a visual message; these forms are *eye*, *painting* and *see*.

### 4.1   Using *eye* to support VISUAL

(37)   Vincent kept his mouth shut and **looked** with big **eyes** at his mother. Never before had he noticed how much skin she had.   (*The Crystal Song*)

*Look* is chosen because the message involves Vincent visually attending to his mother. First, we may observe that the modification *with big eyes*, along with the use of *notice*, provide support for ATTENTION. Second, *eye* is clearly chosen to suggest a message involving visual perception, thus supporting VISUAL. Because *look*, by hypothesis, is also chosen to suggest a message feature of visual perception, this is one aspect of the message to which the two forms – *look* and *eye* – both contribute. It is predicted, therefore, that *look* will co-occur with *eye* at a higher than chance frequency.

For this prediction, the form *hand* will serve as the control term. The prediction is, then, that *look* will favor *eye* in comparison to *hand*. The following COCA searches are carried out (Table 23).

**Table 23.**   COCA searches for *eye* and *hand*

|  | Sequence | Tokens |
|---|---|---|
| Favored | [look] with * [eye] | 29 |
| Disfavored | [look] with * [hand] | 0 |

(*Eye* and *hand* are put in square brackets to allow for both singular and plural forms; the asterisk is a wild-card allowing for any word or punctuation mark). Table 24 presents the results.

**Table 24.**  Total COCA occurrences of *eye* and *hand* in the presence and absence of *look*

|          | *look* present |     | *look* absent |     |
|----------|------|------|--------|------|
|          | N    | %    | N      | %    |
| *eye*    | 29   | 100  | 196765 | 42   |
| *hand*   | 0    | 0    | 275885 | 58   |
| Total    | 29   | 100  | 472650 | 100  |

p < .0001

As is evident in Table 24, *eye* accounts for merely 42 percent of the *eye-hand* total in the absence of *look*. In the presence of *look*, however, there are no occurrences of *hand*, and *eye* accounts for 100 percent of the cases. It may be noted that the same prediction is confirmed (tests run on background) when, instead of *hand*, other control terms are used, such as *ear, nose, tongue,* etc.

## 4.2    Using *painting* to support VISUAL

(38)    There are also painters like El Greco and Jan Vermeer, who [...] produced one or two anomalous but remarkable meteorological landscapes. [... ] Next time you visit an art museum, use your meteorological eye. Scrutinize the painted skies as you would scan the real sky when looking for weather signs. This is a legitimate way to **look** at **paintings**, for the great artists created their skies lovingly and with great care. # Photo: THE CRUCIFIXION, c. 1435 (attributed to Jan van Eyck) is the closest thing to a cloud atlas in the history of art.                    (*Weatherwise; the Sky in Art*)

*Look* is chosen in this example because the writer wants to encourage the reader to visually attend to the skies found in paintings. Note the contextual evidence in support of the hypothesis. First, both *scrutinize* and *scan* support ATTENTION. Second, *meteorological eye* clearly supports VISUAL. Finally, the word *painting* itself also suggests that visual perception is at issue because paintings are objects that people perceive through the sense of sight. This is in contrast to, say, music, which is experienced through auditory perception, rendering *music* a good control term for our next prediction.

It is predicted, then, that *look* will favor *painting* in comparison to *music*. This is because *painting* suggests that visual perception is at issue and *look* is chosen in response to a message that concerns visual perception. The COCA searches are as follows (Table 25).

**Table 25.**  COCA searches for *painting* and *music*

|            | Sequence                  | Tokens |
|------------|---------------------------|--------|
| Favored    | *[look] at [painting]*    | 230    |
|            | *[look] at * [painting]*  |        |
| Disfavored | *[look] at [music]*       | 64     |
|            | *[look] at * [music]*     |        |

**Table 26.**  Total COCA occurrences of *painting* and *music* in the presence and absence of *look*

|            | *look* present |     | *look* absent |     |
|------------|----------------|-----|---------------|-----|
|            | N              | %   | N             | %   |
| *painting* | 230            | 78  | 42109         | 26  |
| *music*    | 64             | 22  | 118090        | 74  |
| Total      | 294            | 100 | 160199        | 100 |

p < .0001

In the absence of *look*, *painting* accounts for merely 26 percent of the *painting-music* total. In the presence of *look*, however, *painting* has significantly increased to 78 percent.

It is of interest to observe that *music* does sometimes co-occur with *look*, and when it does then each form contributes to different and non-overlapping communicative effects. Consider Example (39).

(39)   In July, Tower will test a digital kiosk at its store in Berkeley, Calif., where consumers can have digital compilations made in the store or have songs downloaded to their MP3 players. "Digital is a major part of our lives now, whether we like it or not," Farrace says. "We **look** at digital **music** as just another configuration, like CDs and cassettes."
        (*USA Today; One band's piracy is another's treasure*)

In this example, *digital music* does not suggest a message feature of visual perception, nor of attention. Thus, the choice to utter *look* does not intersect with anything suggested by the choice to utter *music*. In Chapter 2 it has been argued that *look* contributes its hypothesized meaning even in this example because of the cognitive metaphor that maps vision to intellection. What is important for the present purposes is that while *look* contributes to a message of visual (or intellectual) attention, *music* contributes to other message features entirely; therefore, no favoring is predicted between these two forms, as has been confirmed in the counts presented in Table 26.

It is lastly worth mentioning here that this quantitative prediction is indicative of a great number of potential predictions that can be made in light of an analysis of other attested examples. Thus, whenever an example of *look* involves an object that is visually perceived, it may be predicted that *look* will favor the form referring to that visible entity in comparison to another form that indicates a non-visible entity. For instance, much like *look* favors *painting* in comparison to *music*, it may also be predicted that *look* will favor *statue* in comparison to *symphony*, or again, *tree* in comparison to *idea*, etc. While examples of *look at the trees* and *look at this idea* have been observed and analyzed, for ease of presentation we present here only the quantitative data that follows from these examples. Observe, then, that *look* indeed favors *tree* in comparison to *idea* (Tables 27 and 28).

**Table 27.** COCA searches for *tree* and *idea*

|            | Sequence                      | Tokens |
|------------|-------------------------------|--------|
| Favored    | *[look]* [up to 2 slots] *[tree]* | 224    |
| Disfavored | *[look]* [up to 2 slots] *[idea]* | 144    |

**Table 28.** Total COCA occurrences of *tree* and *idea* in the presence and absence of *look*

|       | *look* present | | *look* absent | |
|-------|------|-----|--------|-----|
|       | N    | %   | N      | %   |
| *tree*  | 224  | 61  | 76491  | 35  |
| *idea*  | 144  | 39  | 141298 | 65  |
| Total   | 368  | 100 | 217789 | 100 |
| $p < .0001$ | | | | |

The explanation for these highly significant statistical tendencies is that *look* and a form that is indicative of a visual entity (such as *painting* or *tree*) together contribute to the same visual aspect of the message because, by hypothesis, VISUAL figures in the meaning of *look*.

## 4.3   Using *see* to support VISUAL

(40)   When Ralphie woke the next morning he forgot how he had gotten home.
       He stumbled from bed to **look** and **see** if the car was in the yard.
                                              (*Those Who Hunt the Wounded Dawn*)

In this example, *look* is chosen because the message involves Ralphie directing his visual attention to the yard for the purpose of checking whether the car is there (thus supporting ATTENTION). Support for VISUAL is evidenced in the use of *see*, which is also chosen for its contribution to a message of visual perception. Thus, the speaker's reason for choosing *see* partially intersects with the reason for choosing *look*, both forms contributing to a visual feature of the message. Indeed, Chapter 4 outlines the hypothesized meaning of *see*, which, like *look*, also includes VISUAL in it. It is predicted, then, that *look* and *see* will co-occur at a higher than chance frequency. The form *say* will serve as the control term for this prediction.[30]

**Table 29.**  COCA searches for *see* and *say*

|  | Sequence | Tokens |
|---|---|---|
| Favored | *[look] and [see]* | 366 |
| Disfavored | *[look] and [say]* | 185 |

**Table 30.**  Total COCA occurrences of *see* and *say* in the presence and absence *look*

|  | *look* present | | *look* absent | |
|---|---|---|---|---|
|  | N | % | N | % |
| *see* | 366 | 66 | 805435 | 27 |
| *say* | 185 | 34 | 2197350 | 73 |
| Total | 551 | 100 | 3002785 | 100 |
| $p < .0001$ | | | | |

In the absence of *look*, *see* accounts for 27 percent of the *see-say* total. In the presence of *look*, however, *see* now rises to 66 percent of the total.

## 5.   Conclusion

This chapter has argued that the hypothesized meaning ATTENTION, VISUAL can successfully explain the occurrences of *look* in naturally produced texts of both speech and writing throughout a massive corpus. Each qualitative analysis has

---

**30.**   The reason the control term here is not *hear*, which might appear as a more obvious choice, is that, while *hear* certainly does not contribute the notion of visual to the message, it might contribute a notion of attention, as in, say, *hear me out*. Further investigation of the semantic contribution of the forms *hear*, *listen* (and perhaps *sound*) would be required to tell what precisely is contributed by each one of these. Still, it may be noted that the test with *hear* has been run on background, and the result is that *look* favors *see* also in comparison to *hear*.

argued that the hypothesized meaning ATTENTION, VISUAL has motivated the speaker or writer's expressive choice to utter a token of the form *look*. In each qualitative analysis, a certain form – the predictive term – has been isolated in the text to serve as a surrogate for the suggestion of a certain message effect that – if the meaning hypothesis for *look* is correct – is also contributed by *look*. Then, to make a quantitative prediction, a control term has been selected, one whose expressive choice is motivated by message effects that are completely different and non-overlapping with the message effects contributed by *look*. The quantitative predictions have all confirmed that *look* consistently favors the predictive term in comparison to the control term because the predictive term and, by hypothesis, the meaning of *look* each contribute to partially overlapping message effects. These predictions indirectly support the meaning hypothesis because the communicative strategies tested for – that is, the suggestion of a message partial of attention and of visual – follow from the hypothesized meaning. Finally, for some of the cases, it has been demonstrated that there is nothing incoherent in putting together the two disfavored forms, such as, for instance, *look carelessly* and *look accidentally*. It is just that when these sequences occur, each form is chosen to produce different and non-overlapping communicative effects.

# CHAPTER 4

# ATTENTION, VISUAL in competition with the meanings of *see*, *seem*, and *appear*

## 1. Introduction

This chapter investigates the semantic parameters that guide a speaker's choice to use either *look* or one of the forms *see*, *seem* or *appear*. The tentative hypotheses of *see*, *seem* and *appear* will be elaborated in Sections 2, 3 and 4, respectively. Here in brief, the hypotheses are as follows.

- The meaning of *see* involves an event of registering or internalizing visual sensory input.
- The meaning of *seem* involves a particular perspective or point of view.
- The meaning of *appear* involves the turning point at which something first becomes available to perception.[31]

The interest in comparing *look* to these forms in particular stems from the fact that where these forms occur, *look* is sometimes – on the basis of its hypothesized meaning – an unchosen expressive alternative. This is so because of certain similarities – shared conceptual elements – between the meaning of *look* and the meaning of each of these other forms. To begin with the most straightforward case, *look* and *see* share VISUAL in their meanings, and both may be chosen for a message involving visual perception (e.g., *I saw the painting*; *I looked at the painting*). The two forms differ, by hypothesis, in that only *look* conceptualizes attention in the visual act while only *see* conceptualizes the registering and internalization of visual sensory input. Accordingly, the suggestion of the notion of attention on the one hand and of registering on the other, constitute the semantic parameters that guide a speaker's choice between *look* and *see*.

---

31. A full analysis of *appear* would be necessary to determine whether cases such as *the band is appearing at the theater next week* represent the same form as occurs in *he appears to be innocent*. The analysis here will focus on instances of *appear* like the latter, where *look* is a plausible alternative; the form *appearance* is considered, too.

Second, *look* and *seem* do not formally share, by hypothesis, any notional content in their respective meanings. The two forms, however, functionally converge in that the meanings of both may lead to message partials involving a judgment or opinion. In the case of *look*, the act of attending to something, whether visually or intellectually, may often lead one to form some judgment or opinion about that object of attention (e.g., *I noticed it looks weird*); indeed, the motivation for paying attention to something is often precisely to come to some judgment or opinion about it. In the case of *seem*, the notion of perspective in its hypothesized meaning suggests a particular way or point of view for regarding something; in other words, perspective implies a personal judgment or opinion about something (e.g., *to me it seems obvious*). Because both meanings may lead to inferences involving the idea of a judgment, both *look* and *seem* suit messages of attribution, that is, messages that convey some judgment whose source is conceptualized either as stemming from visual attention (*look*) or from a particular perspective (*seem*). The semantic parameters that will be used to differentiate between the choice of *look* and *seem* will be the notion of visual on the one hand and of perspective on the other.

Finally, the meaning of *appear* fits messages of attribution, too, particularly when the attribution is based on an initial perception. *Look* and *appear* differ, by hypothesis, in that only *appear* contains the notion of initiation, which may be used to suggest that an attribution is tentative and subject to subsequent change (e.g., *it appears white but actually has a semi-translucent color*). Furthermore, both *look* and the derived form *appearance* are fit for messages concerning visual features, but the two forms differ in that only *look* characterizes the visual features as attention-grabbing or attention-worthy while only *appearance* delimits the perception to INITIAL, which may, again, be used to suggest that the characterization of the visual features is provisional (e.g., *please pardon our appearance during construction* – where the current visual features will change as construction takes place).

Each section below presents contrasting pairs of examples that illuminate why *look* is chosen in some cases and why each of the other forms is chosen in others. Most of the qualitative analyses will lead to quantitative predictions, following the same methodology that has been delineated in Chapter 3. Note that, in this chapter, *look* itself will sometimes function as a control term; that is, whenever the predictive term is contributing to a conceptual fragment of the message that is also contributed by *see*, *seem* or *appear* then *look* will serve as the control.[32]

---

32. Forms other than *look* may also serve as control terms in testing the hypotheses of *see*, *seem* and *appear*. For our purposes, however, using *look* as a control term serves to

For instance, in the course of the analysis of Example (46) below, the presence of *believe* will be offered as evidence for the hypothesized meaning of *see*; then, to test the prediction that *believe* and *see* co-occur at a higher than chance frequency, *look* will be used as the control term, so that *see* will be predicted to favor *believe* more so than *look*. Conversely, when the predictive term serves as a surrogate for a semantic parameter that is contributed by *look*, then in that case either *see*, *seem* or *appear* will serve as the control term. For instance, in the course of the analysis of Example (44), the presence of *notice* will be offered as evidence for the meaning of *look*; then, to test the prediction that *notice* and *look* co-occur at a higher than chance frequency, *see* will be used as the control term. In this way, each section below will demonstrate how the choices made by speakers on the basis of the semantic parameters differentiating (by hypothesis) *look*, *see*, *seem* and *appear* are responsible for creating the distributional facts observed in texts.

The reader is reminded that while *look* and *notice* are often chosen to produce a similar effect on the message when they co-occur, they may sometimes be chosen for reasons independent of one another (e.g., *I said I never notice these things. She looked at me blankly…*). By contrast, *see* and *notice* are always chosen for independent reasons and hence are expected to co-occur no more frequently than the null hypothesis would predict. It is this difference between 'sometimes' and 'always' that produces the statistical favoring of *look* and *notice* compared to *see* and *notice*.

Two final preliminary notes are in order. First, when we say that where *see*, *seem* or *appear* occur, *look* might also have occurred, we are not talking of structural substitution; that is, our interest in the comparison is not in the fact that, say, either *look* or *seem* may occur in the empty slot in the frame *She _____ nice*. In the context of the present analysis, the possibility of structural substitution is seen as an epiphenomenon, a consequence of the hypothesized meanings and their fit for particular types of messages, here messages of attribution, as explained above. The goal here, to repeat, is not to explain structural substitution, but rather to explain individual expressive choices; that is, to explicate why a particular form has been chosen on each occasion of use.

Finally, it is outside the scope of this research to offer a full account of the distributions of *see*, *seem* and *appear*, as has been done for *look*. The hypotheses for these other forms are put forth only so as to provide further support for the meaning of *look* by comparing it to these other meanings and explaining both why *look* occurs where it does and why it fails to occur where it might have been expected in light of its hypothesized meaning.

---

explicate why this form is not chosen where – given its hypothesized meaning – we might have expected it.

## 2.  *Look* and *see* – ATTENTION, VISUAL versus EXPERIENCING VISUALLY

This section focuses on the contrast between *look* and *see*. Two terms – *turn to* and *notice* – are shown to be chosen in response to a message feature of attention and so are predicted to be favored by *look* more so than by *see*. This supports the claim that *look* and *see* differ by a feature of attention. Then, we turn to three terms – *believe, understand* and the meaning LESS CONTROL – that are chosen in response to a message feature of perceptual registering or internalization of stimuli, and are predicted to be favored by *see* more so than by *look*. This supports the claim that *look* and *see* differ by a feature of experiencing.

### 2.1   The hypothesis for *see* as a monosemic sign

The hypothesized meaning of *see* involves two notions, the first of which, EXPERI-ENCING, expresses a conceptualization of an event in which visual stimuli make an impression on one's mind; that is, the notion of experience is intended to encapsulate the following concepts: registering, internalizing, processing, being aware of or consciously taking in visual stimuli. The other notion, VISUAL, expresses a conceptualization of the physical sense of sight, as it does in *look*. As in the case of *look*, the two notions make up a single semantic substance, which may be more fully stated as *registering and internalizing visual sensory input*. This hypothesis is summarized in Figure 2.

| Meaning | Signal |
|---|---|
| EXPERIENCING VISUALLY | /si/ or *see* |

Figure 2.  The hypothesis for *see* as a monosemic sign

As a simple initial demonstration, consider the following example.

(41)   [Tour guide:] If you **look** to your right you'll **see** the Empire State Building.

*Look* is chosen because the guide is instructing the tourists to direct visual attention to their right (*to your right* providing contextual support for ATTENTION); *see* is chosen because, as a result of having directed their attention, the tourists will have visually experienced the Empire State Building, that is, register the building through the sense of sight (the meaning LESS CONTROL signaled for *the Empire State Building* provides contextual support for EXPERIENCING, as will be explicated in Section 2.3.3 below).

## 2.2    ATTENTION as the explanation for the choice of *look* over *see*

### 2.2.1    *Using* turn to *to support* ATTENTION

(42)    People **turned to look** at Howard Roark as he passed. Some remained
staring after him with sudden resentment. They could give no reason for it:
it was an instinct his presence awakened in most people. Howard Roark **saw**
no one. For him, the streets were empty. He could have walked there naked
without concern.    (*The Fountainhead*)

Why did the author not write *People turned to* <u>see</u> *Howard Roark as he passed* and
*Howard Roark* <u>looked</u> *at no one*, that is, why did the author make the expressive
choices that she did? The meaning hypotheses explain each of these choices, as
follows. To begin with *look*, note the contextual evidence that attention is a feature
of the communicated message. First, people *turned to* look, implying that people
took special notice of Roark. Further, people *remained staring after him*, suggesting that Roark's presence is quite enthralling; indeed, it *awakens an instinct in most
people*. Finally, a wider contextual consideration relevant to explaining the choice
of *look* is the following: Howard Roark is the protagonist, and so, in the text quoted
in (42), which appears quite at the beginning, the use of *look* – due to its hypothesized meaning – serves to establish Roark as a prominent character to whom
attention ought to be directed. Thus, as evidenced by the use of *turned to* as well as
the other contextual features, we see that this is a message involving attention, and
the writer chose *look* rather than *see* because ATTENTION figures in the meaning of
*look*, whereas *see* contains no element of attention in its meaning.

Turning now to the author's choice of the meaning EXPERIENCING VISUALLY
in *Howard saw no one*. The author chose *see* because the communicated message
is that Howard does not register other people, so much so that *for him, the streets
were empty*, allowing him to *have walked [the streets] naked without concern*.
Larger contextual features again further support the choice of *see*; for instance, a
few paragraphs following this passage, the author writes of Howard that *he made
people feel as if they did not exist*, this again indicating that Howard fails to register
or acknowledge other people. Indeed, Howard's character is throughout the novel
portrayed as an extreme individualist who strictly follows his own path without
allowing anyone to influence his decisions or choices in any aspect of his life.[33] The
message thus concerns more than mere visual perception; Howard generally fails
to acknowledge other people.

---

**33.**    This may read as if it were a literary analysis, but in fact it is a highly rigorous linguistic
analysis, highlighting relevant contextual considerations that explain the author's choices of
*look* and of *see* and hence support these signs' hypothesized meanings.

If the considerations mentioned above regularly guide speakers in their choice between *look* and *see*, they lead to a quantitative prediction. It is predicted that *look* will favor *turn to* more so than *see*. The use of *turn to*, through its suggestion of actively directing, contributes to a message feature of attention, as does the use of *look*. To test this prediction, the total number of occurrences is collected for each of the following six sequences in COCA.

**Table 31.**  COCA searches for *turn to*

|  | Sequence | Tokens |
|---|---|---|
| Favored | *[turn] to look* | |
| | *[turn] * head to look* | 1639 |
| | *[turn] * face to look* | |
| Disfavored | *[turn] to see* | |
| | *[turn] * head to see* | 1010 |
| | *[turn] * face to see* | |

**Table 32.**  Total COCA occurrences of *look* and *see* in the presence and absence of *turn to*

| | *turn to* present | | *turn to* absent | |
|---|---|---|---|---|
| | N | % | N | % |
| *look* | 1639 | 62 | 638695 | 44 |
| *see* | 1010 | 38 | 804791 | 56 |
| Total | 2649 | 100 | 1443486 | 100 |
| $p < .0001$ | | | | |

The prediction is confirmed. The right column shows that in the neutralized condition *look* accounts for 44 percent of the *look-see* total. In the context of *turn to*, however, *look* is clearly favored, constituting now 62 percent of the total. The greater frequency of *turn to look* over *turn to see* is beyond what mere chance would predict. This data confirms the generality of the communicative strategy to utter both *look* and *turn to* so as to suggest a message feature of attention.

As indicated in Table 32, *turn to see* occurs, too. When it does occur, however, each form is chosen for a completely different reason; each contributes to different, non-overlapping message effects. Consider the following example.

(43)    [At a department store:] "That's a gorgeous jean on you," says a voice as I exit my dressing room. I **turn to see** a glam soccer mom awaiting her teenage princess.

(*Harper's Bazaar magazine: Finding the perfect jeans*)

In (43), *turn to* still contributes to a message feature of active directing, but *see* does not. *See* was chosen because the motivation to turn was not to observe a particular person or object of attention, but rather, it was simply to identify an unfamiliar voice. The perception or registering of *a glam soccer mom* was an incidental consequence of doing that, not the actual reason for the turning.

This rationale for *see* rather than *look* finds support in the fact that the writer uses *a* preceding *glam soccer mom*. The meaning of *a* – DIFFERENTIATION REQUIRED yet INCOMPLETE (Reid 1991: 79) – suggests that the writer had no idea what particular visual stimulus she was about to register by turning, implying, thereby, that she did not turn in order to observe the glam soccer mom. By contrast, in Example (42) people turned specifically to observe Howard Roark: *People turned to look at Howard Roark as he passed.* In other words, people first had a visual experience of Howard *as he passed* and then proceeded to orient their eyes in order to visually attend to him.

This rationale for *see* rather than *look* in Example (43) is supported quantitatively through a count checking for the total number of occurrences of the form *a* following *turn to look* and *turn to see*. It is predicted that *turn to see* will favor *a* more so than *turn to look*. The following COCA searches were carried out.

**Table 33.** COCA searches for *turn to a*

|  | Sequence | Tokens |
|---|---|---|
| Favored | *[turn] to see a* | 117 |
| Disfavored | *[turn] to look * a* | 10 |

**Table 34.** Total COCA occurrences of *turn to look* and *turn to see* in the presence and absence of *a*

|  | *a* present | | *a* absent | |
|---|---|---|---|---|
|  | N | % | N | % |
| *turn to see* | 117 | 92 | 840 | 36 |
| *turn to look* | 10 | 8 | 1490 | 64 |
| Total | 127 | 100 | 2457 | 100 |
| $p < .0001$ | | | | |

Whereas *turn to see* accounts for merely 36 percent of the *turn to look*-*turn to see* total, in the context of *a*, *turn to see* now accounts for 92 percent of the total. This favoring of the co-occurrence of *turn to see* and *a* is due to the fact that the reason for the choice of *a* partially overlaps with the reason for the choice of *turn to see*:

both contribute to a message partial involving a turning of one's eyes that is unmotivated by an expectation of what is about to be observed.[34]

### 2.2.2   Using notice to support ATTENTION

There are many more predictive terms suggestive of the notion of attention. Indeed, quantitative tests involving all of the predictive terms examined in Section 3 of Chapter 3 – *carefully, this, but, at, deliberately* and *think* – have been run on background and it has been confirmed that *look* favors each and every one of these forms more so than *see*, thus supporting the presence of ATTENTION in the meaning of *look* and its absence in the meaning of *see*. For ease of presentation, however, and to avoid unnecessary repetition, this data will not be shown here. It will suffice to point to one more predictive term – *notice* – to demonstrate that the choice of *look* over *see* is motivated by the suggestion of a message feature of attention (Example 44 repeats data from the previous chapter, used here for a different purpose).

(44)   He [Peter Keating] tried not to **notice** the faces of the people he passed, but he had to **notice**; he had always **looked** at people.

(45)   [Describing the feats of a man in a wheelchair:] Day one, Waddell climbed three thousand vertical feet in seven and a half hours. Expedition porters used boards to help him tackle the deep drainage ditches in his path. Day two is brutal. Waddell pedals for ten and a half hours to rise thirty three hundred feet in a dust storm. Day three, he covers nearly ten miles. CHRIS-WADDELL: It was really, really tough and steep and loose and rocky. KAREN-BROWN: What drives Waddell [is] his desire that the world stop **seeing** the wheelchair and **notice** the man. CHRIS-WADDELL: I want them to **see** the possibilities in me and people like me. But I also want them to **see** the possibilities in themselves.          (*CBS News Evening*)

First, in regard to Example (44), note now that Peter is portrayed in the novel as having the exact opposite characteristics from Howard. Whereas Howard is a self-made man and an extreme individualist, Peter heavily relies on other people, constantly needing others to tell him what to do and think and seeking other's approval. The author chose here the meaning of *look* because the message involves Peter constantly directing his attention toward other people. This is also conveyed through the use of *notice*, the two forms – *look* and *notice* – together contributing to a message feature of attention.

When *notice* occurs in the presence of *see*, by contrast, then each form is chosen to produce different and non-overlapping message effects. The use of *notice* in

---

34.   Of course, *turn to see* involves three independent expressive choices – of *turn*, of *to* and of *see*. The sequence is treated here as if it were a single choice purely for methodological purposes, in order to show that the overall effect on the message produced by *turn to see* partially overlaps with the effect of *a*.

(45) is still motivated by the suggestion of a message feature of attention; Waddell's desire is that people will actively think of him and attend to him as a capable man. The use of *see*, however, suggests not a notion of attention but one of experiencing; Waddell uses the meaning EXPERIENCING VISUALLY because he wants people to stop registering just the wheelchair. Indeed, through his amazing travels, Waddell strives to make people recognize more in him than might strike one superficially. What is important is that *see* is motivated not by the suggestion of visual attention but by a message that concerns what people visually internalize, or register, when they perceive a man in a wheelchair.

Following these examples, it is predicted that *look* will favor *notice* more so than *see*. To test this prediction, the following COCA searches are carried out.

**Table 35.** COCA searches for *notice*

|            | Sequence                              | Tokens |
|------------|---------------------------------------|--------|
| Favored    | *[look]* [up to 3 slots] *and [notice]* | 125    |
| Disfavored | *[see]* [up to 3 slots] *and [notice]*  | 11     |

**Table 36.** Total COCA occurrences of *look* and *see* in the presence and absence of *notice*

|        | *notice* present | | *notice* absent | |
|--------|------|-----|---------|-----|
|        | N    | %   | N       | %   |
| *look* | 125  | 92  | 640209  | 44  |
| *see*  | 11   | 8   | 805790  | 56  |
| Total  | 136  | 100 | 1445999 | 100 |
| p < .0001 |   |     |         |     |

As indicated in Table 36, in the context of *notice*, *look* is strongly favored, accounting for 92 percent of the *look-see* total.

Summing up, the above two quantitative predictions have confirmed the generality of the communicative strategy motivating speakers to choose *look* over *see* in order to produce a message feature of attention. The next subsection points to three predictive terms that favor *see* over *look*.

## 2.3   EXPERIENCING as the explanation for the choice of *see* over *look*

### 2.3.1   *Using* believe *to support* EXPERIENCING

(46)   When Chris went to school he told everybody about the T-Rex, but no one believed him. [...] Chris took [the T-Rex] to the local zoo. [...] One day the class went to visit the zoo. They **saw** the T-Rex **and believed** Chris.

*(News for Kids; Young authors share their holiday stories)*

(47)    You are quite right in saying that the law changes and interpretations of
        the law change. Where you're wrong is where you want the law to go and it
        seems to me that where you want the law to go is to give every community
        the sort of local option to define what is proper for their citizens to read
        and watch and **look** at **and believe** in. [...] If Cincinnati wants people not to
        watch this painting, they can determine it – I don't think so. MR-MacNeil:
        In other words, you're saying that even if a large majority of the citizens
        in Cincinnati don't like that exhibition, they should not be able to prevent
        citizens, perhaps the small number of citizens who do want to go and see it.
                                                                    (*PBS Newshour, 1990*)

In (46), *see* is chosen because the message is that the kids had visually registered or
experienced the T-Rex when they came to stand in front of it, and the meaning of
*see* is, by hypothesis, EXPERIENCING VISUALLY. Contextual support for the meaning EXPERIENCING VISUALLY comes from the choice of *believed*, suggesting that the
T-Rex had become a part of the kids' internalized cognition; in other words, now
that the kids have visually registered the T-Rex they accept its existence as truth
(consider also, in this respect, the well-known saying "*seeing is believing*"). The two
forms, then, *see* and *believe* contribute to a partially overlapping message effect of
internalized cognition.

In (47), by contrast, each of the forms – *look* and *believe* – contributes to a
different message effect. The speaker protests against the idea that the local community should be able to decide what is proper for its people, and makes this
point by gradually evoking higher degrees of control that the law might exert.
The sequence *read, watch, look* and *believe* creates a kind of crescendo, making
the law seem more and more extreme in its degree of control. *Look* is chosen to
suggest that the law would dictate what a person is allowed to give their attention
to. *Believe*, in turn, suggests that the law will even control one's faith and personal
truths, that is, the most extreme level of control over one's most personal internal convictions. The two forms, then, *look* and *believe* contribute each to different
message effects, one involving acts of visual attention and another involving one's
internal cognition.

Following these examples, it is predicted that *see* will favor *believe* more so
than *look*. To test this prediction, the following COCA searches are carried out.

**Table 37.** COCA searches for *believe*

|            | Sequence                             | Tokens |
|------------|--------------------------------------|--------|
| Favored    | *[see]* [up to 2 slots] *and [believe]* | 34     |
| Disfavored | *[look]* [up to 2 slots] *and [believe]* | 10     |

**Table 38.** Total COCA occurrences of *look* and *see* in the presence and absence of *believe*

|  | *believe* present | | *believe* absent | |
| --- | --- | --- | --- | --- |
|  | N | % | N | % |
| *see* | 34 | 77 | 805767 | 56 |
| *look* | 10 | 23 | 640324 | 44 |
| Total | 44 | 100 | 1446091 | 100 |
| p < .01 | | | | |

While *see* accounts for 56 percent of the *look-see* total in the absence of *believe*, it rises to 77 percent of the total in the presence of *believe*. This prediction confirms the generality of the communicative strategy of using both *see* and *believe* to produce a message feature concerning registered information or internalized cognition.

### 2.3.2    *Using* understand *to support* EXPERIENCING

(48)    Rohm paints in the great outdoors. […] "Working directly from life," he says, "is always a better way to **see and understand** color, value, and form."
(*American Artist*)

(49)    Again and again Diehl returns to the importance of simplifying details. He is in awe of Renaissance works that depict books so minutely that every bit of text on a painted page is readable. But the artist doesn't spend his time going into such a fine detail. He states, "My concern is not to paint every word on a page or every pore on an orange but to **look** closely **and understand** exactly how the light and shadow play off the object. It's a fine-tuning of my eye so that I can see the detail clearly and tackle more intricate surfaces". (*American Artist*)

In (48), the writer chose *see* because the message involves the artist visually experiencing nature (*working directly from life* is *a better way* to visually register *color, value and form*). Note that the use of *understand* likewise contributes to a message of taking in and processing the visual information that strikes the artist in the outdoors. Thus, *see* and *understand* partially overlap in their contribution to the message, both forms suggesting the registering and processing of received input.

In Example (49), by contrast, each of the forms *look* and *understand* contributes to different and non-overlapping message effects. The writer chose *look* because the message involves the artist directing his attention to the visual features of an object of interest. Notice that *look* is modified by *closely*, which is suggestive of special care and attention in the visual act. Furthermore, the artist is interested in _exactly_ _how the light and shadow play off the object,_ again indicating that attention to detail is here at issue. Finally, the next sentence says _it's a fine tuning of my eye,_ yet again suggestive of directed visual attention.

The use of _understand,_ on the other hand, does not contribute to a message of visual attention. It suggests, rather, the registering and processing of the visual information attended to. In this respect, the use of _look and understand_ in Example (49) is rather similar to the sequence where _look_ is followed by _see_ in Example (41) where, to recall, the tourists direct their visual attention in order to visually register the Empire State Building; in both cases the act of visual attention is intended to lead to the registering of visual sensory input. Indeed, note the parallel in (49) between the sequence _look and understand_ and the sequence that appears in the following sentence, _It's a fine-tuning of my eye so that I can see the detail clearly;_ as noted _it's a fine tuning of my eye_ suggests a message similar to the one communicated with _look,_ whereas the use of _see the detail clearly_ suggests a messages similar in its effect to the one communicated with _understand._ Thus, we see that the meanings of _see_ and of _understand_ contribute to overlapping message effects while the meanings of _look_ and _understand_ do not.

Following the analysis of these examples, it is predicted that _see_ will favor _understand_ more so than _look._ To test this prediction, the following COCA searches are carried out.

**Table 39.** COCA searches for _understand_

|            | Sequence                                  | Tokens |
|------------|-------------------------------------------|--------|
| Favored    | _[see]_ [up to 2 slots] _and [understand]_ | 117    |
| Disfavored | _[look]_ [up to 2 slots] _and [understand]_ | 32     |

**Table 40.** Total COCA occurrences of _look_ and _see_ in the presence and absence of _understand_

|       | _understand_ present | | _understand_ absent | |
|-------|------|------|---------|------|
|       | N    | %    | N       | %    |
| _see_   | 117  | 79   | 805684  | 56   |
| _look_  | 32   | 21   | 640302  | 44   |
| Total | 149  | 100  | 1445986 | 100  |
| p < .0001 | | | | |

While _see_ accounts for 56 percent of the _look-see_ total in the absence of _understand,_ it comprises 79 percent in its presence. This confirms the generality of the communicative strategy to use both *see* and *understand* to suggest a message feature of registered information.

### 2.3.3   Using LESS CONTROL to support EXPERIENCING

Note now that while *look* conceptualizes attention that is *directed* through the visual track, *see* conceptualized experiencing that is *mediated* through the visual track. In other words, the meaning of *see* has the visual stimulus built into it, because experiencing necessarily involves something being experienced, that is, something that is registered in the visual act. (One can attend even when there is nothing to attend to simply by the active directing of one's eyes and mind, but it is impossible to experience unless there is something being experienced). This points to a most salient difference in the distributions of the two forms, namely, the fact that *see* is much more likely than *look* to occur with the meaning LESS CONTROL (roughly what the grammatical tradition calls a 'direct object'). Consider the following examples.

(50)   [Mrs. Keating is passing a message to Howard Roark:] She [= the dean's secretary] said to tell you that the Dean wanted to **see you** immediately the moment you got back.                                    (*The Fountainhead*)

(51)   I sat down with Rob Kissel and I **looked him** right across the table at the China Club and I said, "Rob, I think Nancy's trying to kill you."
                                                                            (*NBC Dateline*)

In (50), the use of the meaning LESS CONTROL signaled by the form *you* following (rather than preceding) *see* suggests that Howard has some degree of control over bringing about the event of visual experience suggested by the use of *see*. Indeed, the Dean cannot have a visual experience of Howard unless Howard positions himself in front of the Dean's eyes. Accordingly, the use of the meaning LESS CON-TROL conceptualizes the event of visual experience as one where both the Dean and Howard have some degree of responsibility in bringing the event about. Now the form *see* is partially chosen in light of this same message feature, that is, in light of the suggestion that the perceived object plays a controlling role in the visual event. This message feature is suggested by the meaning EXPERIENCING VISUALLY because this meaning necessarily invokes some visual stimulus that is being experienced.

By contrast, when *look* is used with the meaning LESS CONTROL (*him* in 51), then each choice produces different and non-overlapping message effects. LESS CONTROL is still chosen in light of the controlling role of the visually perceived entity in bringing about the visual event. Thus, Rob Kissel has a crucial role in bringing about the speaker's act of visual attention, as the speaker is visually attending to Rob for Rob's benefit, that is, in order to bring him some vital news. The choice of *look*, however, is not made in light of a controlling role to the visual stimulus, but rather to suggest visual attention. Note that the sequence *I sat down with* already suggests that the speaker is visually experiencing Rob Kissel. *Look* is here chosen (as opposed to *see*) because of the gravity of the information that the speaker has for Rob; in other words, the speaker is prompted to conceptualize the event as one of visual attention (*look*) as opposed to a visual experience (*see*) because the interaction between the speaker and Rob is not just another everyday conversation, but one which compels the speaker to sit and seriously attend to Rob.[35]

Following the rationale for *see* in 10 and for *look* in 11 proposed above, it is predicted that *see* will favor co-occurrence with the meaning LESS CONTROL more so than *look*. This is because both EXPERIENCING VISUALLY and LESS CONTROL contribute to a message where there is a controlling role to the visual stimulus in bringing about the visual event, whereas the meaning of *look* does not contribute to such a message partial. To test this prediction, the total number of occurrences is collected for the following sequences in COCA.

**Table 41.** COCA searches for proper nouns and pronouns

|  | Sequence | Tokens |
| --- | --- | --- |
| Favored | *[see] [proper noun]* | 133310 |
|  | *[see] [pronoun]* |  |
| Disfavored | *[look] [proper noun]* | 5402 |
|  | *[look] [pronoun]* |  |

**Table 42.** Total COCA occurrences of *look* and *see* in the presence and absence of a proper noun or pronoun

|  | *proper noun/pronoun* present | | *proper noun/pronoun* absent | |
| --- | --- | --- | --- | --- |
|  | N | % | N | % |
| *see* | 133310 | 96 | 672491 | 51 |
| *look* | 5402 | 4 | 634932 | 49 |
| Total | 138712 | 100 | 1307423 | 100 |
| $p < .0001$ |  |  |  |  |

---

**35.** Linguists who talk about transitive uses of *look* will typically only mention sequences like *look him in the eye*, which is sometimes posited to be a construction (see, e.g., Wierzbicka 1988: 188–9). But it is quite improbable that *looked him right across the table* is an idiom or a construction; at any rate, this sequence has not been mentioned anywhere in the literature. Our hypothesis for the meaning of *look* together with the established CS hypothesis of the system of Degree of Control make it possible to explain this example as well as examples of *look him in the eye* without the need to posit a construction that exists over and above the sign *look*.

As indicated in Table 42, *see* accounts for 96 percent of the *look-see* total in the presence of LESS CONTROL (again, what is traditionally called a direct object), an increase of 45 percentage points from the neutralized condition. While the reader certainly already knew that *see* occurs with LESS CONTROL more frequently than *look*, it is worth stressing that the meaning hypotheses for each of the forms explain *why* this is so. This underscores the fact that a CS analysis aims at explaining the distribution of linguistic forms, rather than just describing their distribution.

### 3.  *Look* and *seem* – ATTENTION, VISUAL versus PERSPECTIVE DEPENDENCY

This section focuses on the contrast between *look* and *seem*. Both of these forms may be used for both visual and non-visual attributions (e.g., *looks green* and *seems green*, *looks logical* and *seems logical* are all found to occur). Likewise, both forms are sometimes found with an expression indicating who makes the attribution (e.g., *looks nice to me* and *seems nice to me*). None of these sequences is incoherent or ungrammatical, and the reader is reminded that the predictions below involve statistical favorings rather than categorical rules.

One term – *green* – is shown to be chosen in response to a message feature of visual, and so is predicted to be favored by *look* more so than by *seem*. This supports the claim that *look* and *seem* differ by a feature of visual. Then, three predictive terms – *logical*, *to me* and *at the time* – are shown to be chosen in response to a message feature of perspective dependency, and so are predicted to be favored by *seem* more so than by *look*. This supports the claim that *look* and *seem* differ by a feature of perspective dependency.

### 3.1  The hypothesis for *seem* as a monosemic sign

The hypothesized meaning of *seem* – PERSPECTIVE DEPENDENCY – expresses a conceptualization of what is said as relative only to a particular mental point of view, or as stemming from some particular attitude or stance. The hypothesis may be more fully stated as *dependency upon a mental state or point of view from which one's experience is categorized or assessed*. This hypothesis is summarized in Figure 3.

| Meaning | Signal |
|---|---|
| PERSPECTIVE DEPENDENCY | /sim/ or *seem* |

Figure 3. The hypothesis for *seem* as a monosemic sign

As an initial demonstration of the difference between *look* and *seem* consider the following two examples, featuring the sequences *seems correct* and *looks correct*.

(52)   [T]o the question "is it easy for you to get interested in new ideas?" [the gifted pupil] answered: "I get interested if it seems to me the idea is correct, and I reject it if I believe the idea is wrong… Perhaps it is not generally correct, but personally for me it **seems correct**. A new idea is great if I feel it in my heart…                                              (*The international handbook on Giftedness*)

(53)   Fix recording of QML visual tests when using a QGL Widget viewport. Center and clip QML startup animation so it **looks correct** in full-screen.
(https://bugreports.qt.io/browse/QTCREATORBUG-2627)

The first thing to note is that in the case of *seem*, the word *correct* applies to something abstract and completely intellectual – an idea – whereas in the case of *look*, by contrast, *correct* applies now to something that is visually perceived, that is, the visual features of the startup animation in full screen. Second, note that *seem* is chosen because the message is that an idea is deemed as *correct* specifically from the perspective of the child (*perhaps it is not generally correct, but personally for me it seems correct*). By contrast, there is no evidence for perspective dependency in the use of *look*. Indeed, information gained through sight is generally regarded as the most objective source of information there is (Sweetser 1990).[36]

## 3.2   VISUAL as the explanation for the choice of *look* over *seem*

### 3.2.1   Using green *to support* VISUAL

(54)   That fall we prepared a bed and planted it with lettuce, but we didn't place the pod on the bed until February. When we shoveled off the snow and uncovered the bed, which we had protected with a scrap of fiberglass, to our surprise the lettuce still **looked green** and edible underneath all that snow.
(*Mother Earth News – American Intensive Solar Gardening*)

(55)   The qualities that the object actually has are entirely irrelevant to the explanation of the subjective difference between our experiences. In order to explain the difference [in our experience], one must advert to a difference in the way the object seems. […] Suppose [Norm] has an experience that **seems green** to him. We can ask whether the experience *really is* green. If

---

36.   It may be argued that because the meaning of *look* suggests a message partial of attention, it also implies perspective, namely the perspective from which attention is coming. But the meaning of *seem*, by hypothesis, explicitly involves perspective and therefore proves a far better fit – a far more effective instrument to use – for the communication of a message partial of perspective. In other words, when the notion of perspective is central to the communicated message, *seem* rather than *look* will be the form of choice.

it is, his experience is represented to him accurately; if it is not, it is represented to him inaccurately.                                    (*Consciousness and Cognition*)

In (54), *look* is chosen to suggest a message involving visual attention; the speaker
has *shoveled off the snow and uncovered the bed* in order to attend to and examine
the condition of the lettuce. The use of *green* supports the claim that visual perception is at issue because, straightforwardly, the color of the lettuce is a property
perceived through the sense of sight.

In (55), by contrast, *seem* is chosen because the message clearly concerns the gap
that exists between reality and people's personal perspectives. While *green* denotes
a visual property in this example as well, here the point is precisely that the color
depends on the individual's personal perspective. Contextual evidence for a message of perspective comes from the sequences *the qualities that the object actually
has are entirely irrelevant, difference between [people's] experiences, to him* and the
statement that one may judge an object as *green* whether it *really is* green or not. It is
thus evident that the message concerns a feature of perspective and, the writer chose
*seem* rather than *look* because the meaning of *seem* is, by hypothesis, PERSPECTIVE
DEPENDENCY, whereas *look* contains no element of perspective in its meaning.

If the rationales for the occurrence of *look* in (54) and *seem* in (55) guide the
choice between these two words generally, then one would expect *look* to favor
*green* more so than *seem*. This, to repeat, is because the choice of *look* is linked
to the choice of *green* semantically: each is partially chosen for the same reason
(a visual message feature); but the choice of *seem* is not linked semantically to that
of *green* and each is chosen for a different reason. It is predicted then that *look* will
favor *green* more so than *seem*. To test this prediction, the following searches are
carried out in COCA.

**Table 43.** COCA searches for *green*

|            | Sequence       | Tokens |
|------------|----------------|--------|
| Favored    | *[look] green* | 68     |
| Disfavored | *[seem] green* | 2      |

**Table 44.** Total COCA occurrences of *look* and *seem* in the presence and absence of *green*

|        | *green* present | | *green* absent | |
|--------|------|-----|--------|-----|
|        | N    | %   | N      | %   |
| *look* | 68   | 97  | 640266 | 72  |
| *seem* | 2    | 3   | 247307 | 28  |
| Total  | 70   | 100 | 887573 | 100 |

p < .0001

*Look* is strongly favored in the context of *green*, accounting for 97 percent of the *look-seem* total. This data indirectly supports the presence of VISUAL in the hypothesized meaning of *look* and its absence in the hypothesized meaning of *seem*.

We have now seen a case where both *look* and *green* contribute to the same visual aspect of a message. There are many examples where *look* and a form denoting a visual attribute together contribute to a visual message element. For ease of presentation, we will show only the quantitative data (without the qualitative analyses) for two more cases, having to do with the forms *white* and *round* (Tables 45 and 46).

**Table 45.** Total COCA occurrences of *look* and *seem* in the presence and absence of *white*

|       | *white* present | | *white* absent | |
|-------|-----|-----|--------|-----|
|       | N   | %   | N      | %   |
| *look*  | 90  | 95  | 640244 | 72  |
| *seem*  | 5   | 5   | 247304 | 28  |
| Total | 95  | 100 | 887548 | 100 |
| p < .0001 | | | | |

**Table 46.** Total COCA occurrences of *look* and *seem* in the presence and absence of *round*

|       | *round* present | | *round* absent | |
|-------|-----|-----|--------|-----|
|       | N   | %   | N      | %   |
| *look*  | 173 | 99  | 640161 | 72  |
| *seem*  | 1   | 1   | 247308 | 28  |
| Total | 174 | 100 | 887469 | 100 |
| p < .0001 | | | | |

## 3.3    PERSPECTIVE DEPENDENCY as the explanation for the choice of *seem* over *look*

### 3.3.1    *Using* logical *to support* PERSPECTIVE

(56)    People who depended on interest income were hurting. [...] So savers and investors turned to bond mutual funds. It **seemed logical** at the time. [...] What could go wrong? Plenty. Interest rates began rising in October 1993, sparking huge bond losses.                                    (*USA Today*)

(57)    I'm [...] a multimedia designer. [...] I like to create as few tabs as possible in the back-office of Umbraco, to keep everything organized for me and my clients. This means that I get myself in trouble whenever I create a tab with

more than one 'category' under it. For example: when I have two text-fields with titles on the homepage, say one 'About us' and 'Team', I could create a tab called 'Text' in the Umbraco back-office, which contains the next fields: About us_Title; About us_Text; Team_Title; Team_Text [the display features have been eliminated here, N.S]. As you can see, this doesn't look too well. It **looks logical** to me as a developer, but it's a lot of unfriendly text to an end-user.
(*https://our.umbraco.org/forum/using/ui-questions/33446-Creating-categories*)

To begin with (56), in contrast to *green*, the characterization of the idea to invest in bond mutual funds as *logical* constitutes a judgment that is clearly not based on the sense of sight. Rather, this abstract attribution is based on multiple and complex financial considerations that must be analyzed and interpreted to be deemed *logical*, and of course, as is well known, people often disagree in the interpretation of such data. *Seem* is here the form of choice because the message involves a judgment that depends on the limited perspective that the investors had *at the time*. Indeed, from the vantage point of the present time, it is known that *interest rates began rising [...] sparking huge bond losses.*

In (57), by contrast, *look* is chosen because the writer, a multimedia designer, is concerned with the visual features of the pages she designs and how people interact with them. While the message certainly involves visual attributes, the use of *logical* suggests a rather more abstract judgment; *logical* is not seen directly in the visual features the same way that *green* is seen in lettuce (Example 54). Indeed, in saying *to me as a developer*, the designer explicitly differentiates between how the visual features of the page are judged by herself as opposed to her clients; that is precisely the reason for her question. *Look* is the attested form because the designer's question quite explicitly concerns the visual characteristics of the text in the page.

Following these examples, it is predicted that *seem* will favor *logical* more so than *look*.[37] The rationale for this prediction is that *logical* alludes to an abstract

---

37. The rationale for why *look* disfavors *logical* may simply be the fact that *logical* is not a visual attribute. If the meaning of *seem* were hypothesized to be something like NON-VISUAL ATTRIBUTION then the favoring of *seem* toward *logical* would be explained equally well. Note, however, that such a hypothesis for *seem* would fail to explain the other co-occurrence favorings that are coming up in the next sections; e.g., it would have nothing to say about why *seem* favors *at the time*. By the same token, the results presented in Table 48 below might have served to support a hypothesis according to which the meaning of *seem* is LOGICALITY; but here too, such a hypothesis would fail to explain why *seem* and *at the time* also co-occur at a higher than chance frequency. The hypothesis for *seem* proposed here can explain (and has led to the discovery of) this and the rest of the predictions presented below.

characterization whose attribution is not straightforward but rather depends on one's personal interpretation and perspective, and this same message feature of perspective is, by hypothesis, contributed by *seem* as well. To test this prediction, the following searches have been carried out in COCA.

**Table 47.** COCA searches for *logical*

|            | Sequence        | Tokens |
|------------|-----------------|--------|
| Favored    | *[seem] logical* | 235    |
| Disfavored | *[look] logical* | 0      |

As indicated in Table 48, *look logical* does not occur in COCA even once, and *seem* accounts for 100 percent of the *look-seem* total in the presence of *logical*. Still, as demonstrated by Example (57), *look* and *logical* may co-occur sometimes. But when these two forms co-occur then each is contributing to a different message effect.

**Table 48.** Total COCA occurrences of *look* and *seem* in the presence and absence of *logical*

|        | *logical* present | | *logical* absent | |
|--------|-------|-----|--------|-----|
|        | N     | %   | N      | %   |
| *seem* | 235   | 100 | 247074 | 28  |
| *look* | 0     | 0   | 640334 | 72  |
| Total  | 235   | 100 | 887408 | 100 |

p < .0001

It may again be noted that there are many examples where the choice of both *seem* and another form denoting an abstract or intellectual attribute is made in response to a message feature of perspective dependency. Again, for ease of presentation, we will show only the quantitative data for two more cases involving the forms *inevitable* and *reasonable* (Tables 49 and 50).

**Table 49.** Total COCA occurrences of *look* and *seem* in the presence and absence of *inevitable*

|        | *inevitable* present | | *inevitable* absent | |
|--------|-------|-----|--------|-----|
|        | N     | %   | N      | %   |
| *seem* | 253   | 95  | 247056 | 28  |
| *look* | 14    | 5   | 640320 | 72  |
| Total  | 267   | 100 | 887376 | 100 |

p < .0001

**Table 50.** Total COCA occurrences of *look* and *seem* in the presence and absence of *reasonable*

|  | *reasonable* present | | *reasonable* absent | |
|---|---|---|---|---|
|  | N | % | N | % |
| *seem* | 518 | 97 | 246791 | 28 |
| *look* | 14 | 3 | 640320 | 72 |
| Total | 532 | 100 | 887111 | 100 |
| p < .0001 | | | | |

### 3.3.2   *Using* to me *to support* PERSPECTIVE

While of course there are many examples that feature the sequence *seem/look to me*, for ease of presentation we return to Examples (52) and (57), repeated below as (58) and (59), respectively.

(58)   "I get interested if it **seems to me** the idea is correct, and I reject it if I believe the idea is wrong… Perhaps it is not generally correct, but personally **for me it seems** correct.

(*The international handbook on Giftedness*)

(59)   It **looks** logical **to me** as a developer, but it's a lot of unfriendly text to an end-user.

(*https://our.umbraco.org/forum/using/ui-questions/33446-Creating-categories*)

As noted in the analysis above, evidence for the choice of *seem* in (58) comes from the use of *to me*, as well as *personally for me*, these sequences both suggestive of a message feature of perspective dependency, to which the meaning of *seem*, by hypothesis, contributes as well. In Example (59), by contrast, while *to me* still suggests perspective dependency, *look* is motivated by the suggestion of visual attention, as has been analyzed above. Following these examples, it is predicted that *seem* will favor *to me* more so than *look*.[38] To test this prediction, the following searches are carried out in COCA.

---

**38.**   This prediction might have been made if the meaning hypothesized for *seem* were PERSPECTIVE UNDERSPECIFIED while the meaning proposed for *look* were PERSPECTIVE SPECIFIC TO SPEAKER. But such hypotheses would not be able to explain all the other predictions that the hypotheses proposed here have discovered and explained.

**Table 51.** COCA searches for *to me*

|  | Sequence | Tokens |
|---|---|---|
| Favored | *[seem] to me* | |
| | *to me, it [seem] [adj.]* | |
| | *to me it [seem] [adj.]* | 8591 |
| | *[seem] [adj.] to me* | |
| Disfavored | *[look] to me* | |
| | *to me, it [look] [adj.]* | |
| | *to me it [look] [adj.]* | 865 |
| | *[look] [adj.] to me* | |

As shown in Table 52 below, in the presence of *to me*, *seem* accounts for a full 91 percent of the *look-seem* total, an increase of 64 percentage points from the baseline condition.

**Table 52.** Total COCA occurrences of *look* and *seem* in the presence and absence of *to me*

|  | *to me* present | | *to me* absent | |
|---|---|---|---|---|
|  | N | % | N | % |
| *seem* | 8591 | 91 | 238718 | 27 |
| *look* | 865 | 9 | 639469 | 73 |
| Total | 9456 | 100 | 878187 | 100 |
| p < .0001 | | | | |

Observe now that the prediction is confirmed also for the sequences *seem like* and *look like*. This data is of interest as it suggests that there is no reason to think that *look* or *seem* are chosen on different grounds than the hypotheses proposed here – even when they occur as part of this putative construction.

**Table 53.** COCA searches for *to me* (for *look/seem like*)

|  | Sequence | Tokens |
|---|---|---|
| Favored | *[seem] [up to 3 slots] like to me* | |
| | *[seem] to me like* | 365 |
| Disfavored | *[look] [up to 3 slots] like to me* | |
| | *[look] to me like* | 672 |

**Table 54.** Total COCA occurrences of *look like* and *seem like* in the presence and absence of *to me*

|            | *to me* present | | *to me* absent | |
|            | N   | %   | N     | %   |
|------------|-----|-----|-------|-----|
| *seem like* | 365 | 35  | 15257 | 21  |
| *look like* | 672 | 65  | 56114 | 79  |
| Total      | 1037 | 100 | 71371 | 100 |

p < .0001

While here *seem like* increases by only 14 percentage points in the presence of *to me*, this increase is nonetheless highly statistically significant, as indicated by the low *p* value.

**3.3.3** *Using* at the time *to support* PERSPECTIVE
Example (56), which features *seemed...at the time*, is repeated below as (60); (61) is new.

(60)   People who depended on interest income were hurting. [...] So savers and investors turned to bond mutual funds. It **seemed** logical **at the time**. [...] What could go wrong? Plenty. Interest rates began rising in October 1993, sparking huge bond losses.                                            (*USA Today*)

(61)   LB: What was your biggest fashion mistake? BS: Ten years ago at the Billboard awards, I wore this orange hat and orange bra and orange booty pants and purple fishnets. Oh, and I had an orange jacket on. LB: Was it Halloween? BS laughs: No, it wasn't Halloween. I actually thought I **looked** hot at **the time**. But, um, I definitely stood out.              (*Harper's Bazaar*)

Recall that in Example (60) the use of *at the time* implies a message feature of perspective dependency; the judgment of the investment as logical was made on the basis of the inevitably limited information available at the time. The use of *seem*, by hypothesis, likewise contributes to a message feature of perspective dependency. In Example (61), by contrast, *at the time* still suggests perspective dependency, but the writer chose *look* because the message involves visual attention, as is evidenced by the fact that BS is describing her ensemble on a particular occasion and that she *definitely stood out*. Thus, *look* and *at the time* each contribute to different and non-overlapping message effects; each was chosen for a different expressive reason. It is predicted, then, that *seem* will favor *at the time* more so than *look*. To test this prediction, the following searches are carried out in COCA.

**Table 55.** COCA searches for *at the time*

|  | Sequence | Tokens |
|---|---|---|
| Favored | *[seem]* [up to 3 slots] *at the time* | 337 |
|  | *at the time,* [up to 3 slots] *[seem]* |  |
| Disfavored | *[look]* [up to 3 slots] *at the time* | 102 |
|  | *at the time,* [up to 3 slots] *[look]* |  |

**Table 56.** Total COCA occurrences of *look* and *seem* in the presence and absence of *at the time*

|  | *at the time* present | | *at the time* absent | |
|---|---|---|---|---|
|  | N | % | N | % |
| *seem* | 337 | 77 | 246972 | 28 |
| *look* | 102 | 23 | 640232 | 72 |
| Total | 134 | 100 | 887204 | 100 |
| p < .0001 | | | | |

Here we see an almost complete flip toward *seem* in the presence of *at the time*.

## 4.  *Look* and *appear* – ATTENTION, VISUAL versus INITIATION OF PERCEPTION

This section focuses on the contrast between *look* and *appear*. Four terms – *introduce, first, [adjective]-er than*, and *but* – are shown to be chosen in response to a message feature of initiation and so are predicted to be favored by *appear* more so than by *look*. This will support the claim that *look* and *appear* differ by a feature of initiation, as explicated below. Then, some contrasting pairs of examples of *look* and *appearance* will be examined.

### 4.1  The hypothesis for *appear* as a monosemic sign

The hypothesized meaning of *appear* – INITIATION OF PERCEPTION – expresses a conceptualization involving the point of emergence of a stimulus onto a scene. Again, the hypothesis may be more fully stated as *sensory stimuli as they first enter or become available to perception*. This hypothesis is summarized in Figure 4.

| Meaning | Signal |
|---|---|
| INITIATION OF PERCEPTION | /əpir/ or *appear* |

**Figure 4.** The hypothesis for *appear* as a monosemic sign

## 4.2 INITIATION as the explanation for the choice of *appear* over *look*

### 4.2.1 *Using* introduce *to support* INITIATION

(62) It is commonly suggested to correct perspective using a general projective transformation tool, correcting vertical tilt by stretching out the top; this is the "Distort Transform" in Photoshop, and the "Perspective Tool" in GIMP. However, this **introduces** vertical distortion – objects **appear** squat (vertically compressed, horizontally extended) – unless the vertical dimension is also stretched. This effect is minor for small angles, and can be corrected by hand, manually stretching the vertical dimension until the proportions **look** right. (*Wikipedia: Perspective Control*)

Notice, first, that *look* might have occurred in the place where *appear* is attested. *Appear*, however, is here the form of choice because the characterization of the objects as *squat* is only an initial state of affairs, and INITIATION OF PERCEPTION is, by hypothesis, the meaning of *appear*. There are several pieces of contextual evidence indicating that *squat* is only an initial characterization. First, the tool *introduces vertical distortion*, indicating that vertical distortion emerges – and hence, comes to sight – only upon the use of the tool. Second, the sequence *unless the vertical dimension is also stretched* suggests that if this additional procedure is executed then the initial *squat* will no longer obtain. And third, *the effect is minor and can be corrected* suggests yet again that *squat* will not obtain. Thus, the message concerns a feature of initiation and, the writer chose *appear* rather than *look* because the meaning of *appear* is, by hypothesis, INITIATION OF PERCEPTION, whereas *look* contains no element of initiation in its meaning.

Turning now to the use of *look* in the example, here the message clearly involves a visually attending agent, and hence the choice of the meaning ATTENTION, VISUAL. Note that the user must fine-tune the image – *manually stretching* it – until its relevant visual features are deemed to be *right*.[39] This procedure requires the user's visual attention, so that they could tell when the image has achieved its proper dimensions. Further evidence comes from *correct by hand*, which is also indicative of an attending agent.

If the considerations mentioned above regularly guide speakers in their choice between *look* and *appear*, they lead to a quantitative prediction. As noted, the use

---

39. There is of course an initial moment of perception at which the visual features are deemed right. But *look* is a better fit here than *appear* because the communication does not here concern these visual features being provisional in any way; that is, the message is not about the initiation of this perception. Rather, the message does involve the visual features being attended to in order to be deemed as *right*, as explained.

of *introduce* suggests a message feature of initiation in that it alludes to visual features as they first enter onto the scene. *Appear*, by hypothesis, is likewise used to suggest a message feature involving visual properties first entering onto a scene, whereas *look* does not. It is therefore predicted that *appear* will favor *introduce* more so than *look*. To test this prediction, the following searches are carried out in COCA.

**Table 57.**  COCA searches for *introduce*

|  | Sequence | Tokens |
|---|---|---|
| Favored | *[introduce]* [up to 7 slots] *[appear]* | 49 |
| Disfavored | *[introduce]* [up to 7 slots] *[look]* | 105 |

**Table 58.**  Total COCA occurrences of *look* and *appear* in the presence and absence of *introduce*

|  | *introduce* present | | *introduce* absent | |
|---|---|---|---|---|
|  | N | % | N | % |
| *appear* | 49 | 32 | 113160 | 15 |
| *look* | 105 | 68 | 640229 | 85 |
| Total | 154 | 100 | 753389 | 100 |
| p < .0001 | | | | |

*Appear* accounts for merely 15 percent of the *look-appear* total in the neutralized condition. In the presence of *introduce*, however, *appear* now comprises 32 percent of the total, an increase of 17 percentage points. The favoring of *introduce* by *appear* in comparison to *look* confirms that *appear* is regularly used for a message partial of initiation, thus indirectly supporting its hypothesized meaning.

### 4.2.2   *Using* first *to support* INITIATION

(63)   As they entered, the snap of the closing door echoed off the walls of the quiet house. The living room was dimly lit and at **first appeared** empty. Then something stirred across the room, and an opaque figure rose and came forward. Crow switched on the light, exposing a teenage girl, eyes heavily mascaraed, hair overly teased. The distinctive odor of baby powder drew the couple's attention to an infant asleep in her boyish arms.

*(Jitterbug Descending)*

(64)   [A designer explains his philosophy:] "Simplify, then exaggerate," is how he explains his design philosophy. "Have one color, beige, but have 15 shades

of beige. The result at **first looks** simple, but after looking at it a while, you realize there are 15 textures of beige and it's all quite complex."
(*Atlanta Journal Constitution – The Grand Designs of Charles Gandy*)

In (63) *appear* was chosen because the narrative clearly focuses on how the room was perceived initially, preparing the reader for what will be discovered subsequently. Evidence of a message feature concerning only an initial state of affairs comes from the following sequences: *as they entered,* evoking an image of the characters entering a new scene; *the quiet house,* suggesting that the house is probably empty; *at first,* suggesting that subsequent moments will bring the discovery of something new; and finally, following the initially deceptive perception, *an opaque figure rose [...] exposing a teenage girl,* these underlined forms indicating how the figure suddenly entered the character's perception. The author thus chose *appear* rather than *look* because, by hypothesis, the meaning of *appear* contributes to a message involving the initial moment of perception whereas the meaning of *look* does not.

In (64), the use of *first* similarly produces a message effect of an initial state of affairs, suggesting changes in subsequent moments. Here, however, the writer chose *look* because the designs are intended to be noticed and visually attended to. The use of *but after looking at it a while* suggests that, initially, the spectator gives visual attention to the design only briefly, which would lead one to think of the design as *simple,* then a longer act of visual attention would bring one to notice that *it's all quite complex.*

Because *first* and *appear* are chosen to produce a partially overlapping message effect, it is predicted that *appear* will favor *first* more so than *look.* The following searches are carried out in COCA.

**Table 59.** COCA searches for *first*

|  | Sequence | Tokens |
| --- | --- | --- |
| Favored | *first* [up to 3 slots] *[appear]* | 1256 |
| Disfavored | *first* [up to 3 slots] *[look]* | 962 |

**Table 60.** Total COCA occurrences of *look* and *appear* in the presence and absence of *first*

|  | *first* present | | *first* absent | |
| --- | --- | --- | --- | --- |
|  | N | % | N | % |
| *appear* | 1256 | 57 | 111953 | 15 |
| *look* | 962 | 43 | 639372 | 85 |
| Total | 2218 | 100 | 751325 | 100 |
| p < .0001 | | | | |

*Appear* is strongly favored in the context of *first*, accounting for 57 percent of the *look-appear* total. Now some of the results in this search include cases such as *The book first appeared in 1972*, where *look* is not a viable option. Note, however, that even if the search is restricted so that an adjective immediately follows *first look/appear* the prediction is still confirmed. The following searches are carried out in COCA.

**Table 61.** COCA searches for *first-adjective*

|  | Sequence | Tokens |
|---|---|---|
| Favored | *first [appear] [adj.]* | 37 |
|  | *[appear] [adj.] at first* |  |
| Disfavored | *first [look] [adj.]* | 46 |
|  | *[look] [adj.] at first* |  |

**Table 62.** Total COCA occurrences of *look* and *appear* in the presence and absence of *first-adjective*

|  | *first-adjective* present | | *first-adjective* absent | |
|---|---|---|---|---|
|  | N | % | N | % |
| *appear* | 37 | 45 | 113172 | 15 |
| *look* | 46 | 55 | 640288 | 85 |
| Total | 83 | 100 | 753460 | 100 |
| p < .0001 | | | | |

### 4.2.3 Using comparative adjectives to support INITIATION

(65) Objects in mirror are **closer than** they **appear**.

*(posted on the side mirror of vehicles)*

(66) Here are six ways that passenger vehicle motorists can help to keep motorcyclists safe on the roads: [...] 2. It can be tough to judge a motorcycle's speed. Before inching out into an intersection, assume a motorcycle is **closer than** it **looks**. (http://www.vanweylaw.com/blog/motorcycle-safety-lawyer-motorcyclists-deserve-respect-too.cfm)

Beginning with (65), notice again that *look* could have been used here (and *seem* too, for that matter). But *appear* is the form attested and its choice can be explained in light of the hypothesis. At the first moment it is perceived, the object in the mirror may be deemed far; but, in fact, contrary to what the perceiver may initially suppose, it is close. Evidence for a message of initial perception comes from the use of *-er than*, which simultaneously alludes to two different states of affairs; in this case, one which is merely perceived and another which is real. The use of *-er than* thus renders the visual features as only tentative, an initial approximation, and because, by hypothesis, the meaning of *appear* is INITIATION OF PERCEPTION this tentativeness is also here suggested by the use of *appear*. That is, the meaning of *appear* has been chosen because the message involves immediately overriding the given attribution.

In (66), while the use of *-er than* still suggests that the visual features characterized as *close* are possibly only tentative, the use of *look*, by hypothesis, does not. Rather, the writer chose *look* because the theme of the text involves visual attention to motorcyclists on the road, and, by hypothesis, ATTENTION, VISUAL is the meaning of *look*. Contextual evidence for the notion of attention is found in *tough to judge*, which involves an agent directing their attention to the motorcycle in an attempt to *determine* its speed. What is important is that the choice of *look* on the one hand and of *-er than* on the other are each made for different communicative effects.

Following the rationales articulated above, it is predicted that *appear* will favor the sequence *[comparative adjective] than* more so than *look*. The following searches are carried out in COCA.

**Table 63.** COCA searches for comparative adjectives

|  | Sequence | Tokens |
|---|---|---|
| Favored | *[comp. adj.] than * [appear]* | |
| | *more [adj.] than * [appear]* | 132 |
| | *less [adj.] than * [appear]* | |
| Disfavored | *[comp. adj.] than * [look]* | |
| | *more [adj.] than * [look]* | 304 |
| | *less [adj.] than * [look]* | |

**Table 64.** Total COCA occurrences of *look* and *appear* in the presence and absence of comparative adjectives

| | *comp. adj.* present | | *comp. adj.* absent | |
|---|---|---|---|---|
| | N | % | N | % |
| *appear* | 132 | 30 | 113077 | 15 |
| *look* | 304 | 70 | 640030 | 85 |
| Total | 436 | 100 | 753107 | 100 |
| p < .0001 | | | | |

Whereas *appear* accounts for 15 percent of the *look-appear* total in the neutralized condition, in the presence of a comparative adjective *appear* rises to 30 percent of the total. This supports the presence of INITIATION in the hypothesized meaning of *appear* and its absence in the meaning of *look*.

It is worth pointing out that Example (65) – but not (66) – alludes to a kind of optical illusion. Indeed, the meaning of *appear* is suitable for messages involving optical illusions because it specifically concerns the initial moment of visual perception, allowing thereby for the possibility of a different perception at subsequent moments. An optical illusion strikes one as having certain visual features, but because it is an illusion, these visual features do not in fact obtain. For instance, at the initial moment of perception, it may *appear that the sun and the moon are the same size* (example from *Wikipedia, Optical Illusions*), but then this is an illusion, so actually they are not. Indeed, it is of interest to note that, while *look* is by far the more frequent form of the two – occurring in COCA about five times more frequently than *appear*, still, within the *Wikipedia* article *Optical Illusions* (April, 2015) it is the form *appear* that outnumbers *look* by a ratio of three to one.

### 4.2.4   *Using* but *to support* INITIATION

(67)   As semiaquatic rodents, beavers have closable ears and nostrils, webbed hind feet and very dense fur coats. Their paddle-like tails **appear** to be covered in scales like a fish, **but** they aren't. Rather, the skin is grooved in a scaly pattern which makes the thick tail more flexible.
(*Plaque at the American Museum of Natural History*)

(68)   If you can't afford to have garments altered, try different brands or designers until you find the one that fits you perfectly. Small Details Make a Big Difference. Two items of clothing may **look** exactly alike, **but** subtle variations can dramatically alter how it looks on you.   (*Ebony*)

In (67), *appear* is chosen because the message involves a contrast between an initial approximation and a subsequent realization. Evidence for the initial aspect in the message comes from *but they aren't* and *rather*, indicating that the preceding information is only an initial semblance; indeed, recall from Chapter 3 that *but* is used to override information preceding it (Crupi 2004).

In (68), *but* is still used to override the information that precedes it, but *look* is chosen to suggest a message feature of visual attention, which is evidenced throughout the text. First, the text provides fashion advice, a topic clearly associated with attention to visual features. Second, *until you find the one that fits you perfectly* suggests assessment and decision, acts that clearly require conscious thought and attention. Third, *small details* alludes to visual details, and these can *make a big difference* only if someone pays attention to them.

Because, as argued in the analyses above, *appear* and a following *but* together suggest a message concerning an initial approximation, whereas *look* and a following *but* contribute each to non-overlapping message effects, we predict that *appear* will favor a following *but* more so than *look*.[40] The following searches are carried out in COCA.

**Table 65.** COCA searches for *but*

|  | Sequence | Tokens |
|---|---|---|
| Favored | *[appear]* [up to 5 slots] *but* | 778 |
| Disfavored | *[look]* [up to 5 slots] *but* | 2823 |

**Table 66.** Total COCA occurrences of *look* and *appear* in the presence and absence of *but*

|  | *but* present | | *but* absent | |
|---|---|---|---|---|
|  | N | % | N | % |
| *appear* | 778 | 22 | 112431 | 15 |
| *look* | 2823 | 78 | 637511 | 85 |
| Total | 3601 | 100 | 749942 | 100 |
| p < .0001 | | | | |

In the context of a following *but*, *appear* accounts for 22 percent of the *look-appear* total. While this is an increase of only 7 percent from the neutralized condition, as indicated by the *p* value, this favoring is highly significant statistically.

## 4.3 Messages involving visual features: *look* versus *appearance*

We first note that further research is required to determine whether the *appear* in *appearance* is the same signal as in the hypothesis presented in Figure 3 above. For our purposes, we will see that *appearance* can be treated as a derived form that more or less retains the same meaning as *appear*.

Let us compare the expressions in (69) and (70), all attested.

---

40. Note that in Chapter 3 it was predicted that *look* will favor a <u>preceding</u> *but* whereas the prediction now involves a <u>following</u> *but*. In both cases we rely on Crupi's (2004) hypothesis that *but* involves the overriding of preceding information.

(69)   a.   Keeping up **appearances**.
       b.   Please pardon our **appearance** during construction.

(70)   a.   You shouldn't rely on your **looks** to get what you need and want.
       b.   It's the new **look**.

First, *appearance* is chosen in (69) because both of these expressions communicate a message that involves the notion of initiation: *keeping up appearances* is used to refer to a person who consistently wants to maintain the effect of a first impression, never going any deeper but always remaining on the surface; *pardon our appearance* is used for messages involving temporary states of affairs, indicating how the visual features are now, but suggesting, by hypothesis, through the use of *appear*, that they will change soon. By contrast, *look* is chosen in (70) because here both expressions involve attention to visual features. As has already been discussed in Chapter 2, a person who *relies on their looks* expects special treatment from other people, contingent on them noticing (and hence being affected by) the person's visual features. And, when a fashion magazine declares some style to be *the new look*, then the message is that the visual characteristics of this style currently catch the (fashion tuned) public's attention.

The following attested examples provide further evidence for the different communicative effect of *look* and *appearance*, now specifically in alluding to the visual features of someone's face.

(71)   [Dominique's father, Francon, wants to set up a date between Dominique and Peter. Francon invites both Dominique and Peter for a lunch without Dominique knowing of the setup. Dominique begins:] "It was wonderful of you to take time off to see me, Father. Particularly when you're so busy and have so many appointments." **Francon's face assumed a look of consternation.** "My God, Dominique, that reminds me!" "You have an appointment you forgot?" she asked gently. "Confound it, yes! It slipped my mind entirely. Old Andrew Colson phoned this morning and I forgot to make a note of it and he insisted on seeing me at two o'clock, you know how it is, I just simply can't refuse to see Andrew Colson, confound it!--today of all..." He added, suspiciously: "How did you know it?" "Why, I didn't know it at all. It's perfectly all right, Father. Mr. Keating and I will excuse you, and we'll have a lovely luncheon together.                              (*The Fountainhead*)

(72)   [Peter has come over to Katie's apt.] He sat down and stretched out his arm in silent invitation. She came to him promptly, she put her hand in his, and he pulled her down to the arm of his chair. The lamplight fell on him, and she had recovered enough to notice **the appearance of his face**. "Peter," she gasped, "what have you been doing to yourself? You look awful." "Drinking." "Not...like that!" "Like that..." "Darling...what have they done to you?"                              (*The Fountainhead*)

Beginning with (71), the author here chose *look* because Francon is visually attending to Dominique while deliberately and willfully *assuming* a particular facial expression. Note that Francon's *look of consternation* is made for Dominique's sake, that is, it is essential to his plan that Dominique will pay attention to his face as he assumes the expression. His plan works, as indicated by Dominique asking *You have an appointment you forgot?*

By contrast, in (72) there is no evidence that Peter intends for Katie to pay attention to the visual features of his face. Indeed, Peter does not *assume* a facial expression, but rather the visual features of his face are as they are whether or not Katie is paying attention to them. The author chose *appear* because the message involves the visual features of Peter's face suddenly entering Katie's perception. Note the contextual evidence. First, *the lamplight fell on him* suggests that previously Peter was rather in the dark and only now Katie first sees him in a proper light. Second, *she had recovered enough* suggests a message involving how the image of his face is taking shape for her. Lastly, in response to what she suddenly sees, *she gasped*, indicating her shock as she sees Peter's face for the first time.[41] Examples (71) and (72) thus illustrate how the same author sometimes chooses *look* and sometimes *appearance* in response to different intended effects on the message; *look* is chosen because the message concerns attention to visual features while *appearance* is chosen because the message involves visual features first entering one's perception.

We turn now to one final pair of examples, again contrasting *look* and *appearance*, this time both forms used in reference to Dominique.

(73)   [Before Peter has ever seen Dominique] He [= Peter] looked at Francon's squat figure and wondered what **appearance** his daughter must have inherited to earn her father's so obvious disfavor.          (*The Fountainhead*)

(74)   [After Peter has met Dominique for the first time:] "Well?" Francon asked ominously. Keating smiled. "You're a pig, Guy. You don't know how to appreciate what you've got. Why didn't you tell me? She's the most beautiful woman I've ever seen." "Oh, yes," said Francon darkly. "Maybe that's the trouble." "What trouble? Where do you see any trouble?" "What do you really think of her, Peter? Forget the **looks**. You'll see how quickly you'll forget that. What do you think?"          (*The Fountainhead*)

---

41.   Notice that *appearance* is used by the omniscient narrator, describing from an outside perspective how Peter's face suddenly entered Katie's field of vision, whereas Katie herself utters *look awful*. Katie uses *look* because she, in her utterance, communicates a message involving her concerns having visually attended to Peter's face.

Beginning with (73), note first that *look* would seem inappropriate here because inherited visual features are as they are regardless of whether or not anyone is paying attention. The author chose *appearance* because, first, inherited visual features emerge with birth, and further, they are inherently provisional, subject to change throughout one's life. In (74), by contrast, *look* is chosen because Peter has seen Dominique and has clearly paid attention to her visual features. This is evidenced by the fact that he is somewhat upset at Francon because he doesn't *know how to appreciate what* he's got and because he *didn't tell* Peter of her beauty; Peter even exclaims that Dominique is *the most beautiful woman* he has *ever seen*. Lastly, *forget the looks* and *what do you think* are used by Francon to get Peter to quit attending to her visual features and direct attention instead to her personality.

## 5.   Conclusion

This chapter has offered tentative meaning hypotheses for the forms *see, seem* and *appear*. These hypotheses, along with the meaning ATTENTION, VISUAL, explain speakers' expressive choices between *look* and each of these other forms. The forms differ from one another along several semantic parameters, according to their respective meanings. We have seen that *see* and *look* differ on the basis of the semantic parameters of attention and experiencing. When the speaker wants to highlight attention in the visual act then *look* is chosen, and when the speaker wants to highlight the registering of visual stimuli then *see* is chosen. We have also seen that this registering aspect in the meaning of *see* explains its relatively frequent co-occurrence with LESS CONTROL, as both meanings contribute to a message involving a controlling role to the object of perception in bringing about the visual event. Then we have seen that *look* and *seem* differ on the basis of the semantic parameters of visual and perspective dependency. When the message concerns a visual attribute then *look* is chosen; when the message concerns an abstract or intellectual attribution then *seem* is chosen. *Seem* is also chosen when the speaker wants to underscore the attribution as stemming from a particular perspective, as was evidenced by the frequent co-occurrence of *seem* with *to me* and *at the time*. Finally it was demonstrated that *look* and *appear* differ on the basis of the semantic parameters of attention and initiation. We have seen that when the message involves an attribution being tentative or merely an initial approximation then *appear* is chosen. It was lastly shown that in messages involving visual features only *look* may imply that these features are attention-worthy or attention-grabbing.

# CHAPTER 5

# Competing analyses of the meaning of *look*

## 1.  Introduction

The case has been made that the hypothesized meaning ATTENTION, VISUAL successfully explains why *look* occurs where it does in texts, as characterized in both
qualitative and quantitative terms, including why *look* is chosen where *see*, *seem*
and *appear* may initially appear as plausible alternatives. This chapter reviews
three competing proposals of the meaning of *look* and explicates why I believe that
the hypothesis provided here constitutes a more comprehensive explanation of the
distribution of *look* than the other hypotheses found in the literature. In particular,
our hypothesis is the only one that has led to the discovery of new large-scale distributional patterns not previously noticed, much less explained. Throughout this
chapter we will return to some of the themes that were introduced in Chapter 1
and see how these issues impact the analyses of other researchers; these including:
(a) the issue of beginning analysis with the adoption of the a priori grammatical
categories, (b) the issue of limiting one's dataset to sentences constructed by the
analyst, and (c) the issue of identifying the linguistically encoded meaning with
fractions of the interpretive whole.

   Briefly, the analyses to be reviewed are the following. The first proposal comes
from a generative approach to language acquisition presented in Landau and
Gleitman (1985) (henceforth, LG) that offers a componential analysis of the meaning of *look*. The second proposal comes from a constructionist analysis presented in
Wierzbicka (1988) who posits a meaning to the putative construction *have a look*.
Finally, the third proposal comes from a study presented in Tobin (1993) who offers,
as we do, meaning hypotheses to explain the distributions of *look* and *see*. Tobin's
analysis, while akin to a CS-style meaning hypothesis, nonetheless relies, as we will
see, on the notion of markedness – an a priori theoretical apparatus generally not
appealed to in CS hypotheses. Each of these proposals will now be explicated in turn.

## 2.  A componential analysis

LG's analysis of the meaning of *look* is part of a larger enterprise carried in the
spirit of Chomsky's well known argument of the poverty of the stimulus. LG's

essential argument is that external input from speech events provides insufficient evidence for learning a verb's meaning, and so, they propose, the set of subcategorization frames of a verb provides crucial clues for a child to figure out what the meaning of a verb is (1985: 138). Accordingly, each of the syntactic environments within which the verb *look* regularly occurs is taken to be indicative of some aspect of its meaning.

Note that in our analysis as well, we have relied on the linguistic contexts within which *look* regularly occurs to formulate and support our meaning hypothesis. Unlike LG, however, we did not bias our investigation and examine only cases where *look* co-occurs with act or event-suggesting grammatical forms (e.g., *-ed*). Moreover, and as discussed extensively in Chapter 1, we recognize that a hypothesized meaning need not be identified with the messages or message partials that the form is used to communicate. But, because LG do seem to identify the linguistically encoded meaning with the communicated message, they inevitably conclude that, because *look* occurs in multiple syntactic environments, its meaning involves multiple components (1985: 144), each component corresponding to some partial of the message that is communicated in each syntactic environment in which *look* occurs.

First, LG note that *look* is regularly used with locative prepositions, such as *to, into, up, down, back, forward, behind*, etc. Following Gruber (1967), LG appeal to the intuition that, when one looks then one's gaze is moving along a path in the direction indicated by the locative (1985: 128–9). They conclude therefore that one component in the meaning of *look* is 'motion'. In order to distinguish *look* from other 'verbs of motion', such as *come* and *go*, LG posit another meaning component in *look*, 'perceptual'. The subcategorization frame that is hypothesized to facilitate the acquisition of this component of the meaning of *look* is the fact that *look* – unlike *come* and *go* – occurs with 'how-relatives', such as in *look how I do it* (1985: 130). To continue, because both 'motion' and 'perceptual' also figure as components in the meaning proposed for *see*, in order to distinguish *look* from *see* LG note that *look* occurs significantly more frequently than *see* both as an imperative (*Look!*) and in the progressive (*looking*), leading them to posit that yet another component in the meaning of *look* – absent in the meaning of *see* – is 'activity' (1985: 133).

Now when LG come to occurrences of *look* as found in *He looks like a kangaroo*, they seem uncertain whether this presents the same, or a different, lexical entry from the *look* found in cases like *He looked at the picture* (1985: 142–4). The meaning components they posited so far – 'motion', 'perception' and 'activity' – seem to them to be insufficient to explain these uses of *look*, and so they initially propose that *look like* is a special type of construction meaning either 'resemble' or 'appear' (1985: 143). But then they note that a meaning component they call 'inspect by eye' may be seen as applicable to both *He looked at the picture* and to *He looks like a kangaroo* because, even in *He looks like a kangaroo*, an agent inspecting by eye is implicit and can be made explicit with the addition of *to me*. They therefore provisionally conclude that it is the same verb *look* in both cases.

In this work, too, it has been argued that it is the same sign (not verb) *look* in both of these cases. It is of interest to note, however, that the consequence of it being the same *look* in both cases simplifies our analysis yet complicates LG's (which is in fact partially why they are hesitant in proposing it). Our own analysis is simplified because the hypothesis of a single sign has been shown to successfully explain by itself the full range of the distribution of *look*. LG's analysis, by contrast, becomes more complex because now they have the same *look* in quite different syntactic patterns, and "a construal rule of some complexity would be required to relate the surface form required in these cases (patient as subject NP, experiencer as indirect object NP, and so on) [e.g., *He looks like a kangaroo*, N.S] to the more familiar formats [e.g., *He looked at a kangaroo*, N.S] in which *look* participates" (1985: 144). Note the use of the expression "relate… to the more familiar formats", suggesting that for LG some syntactic patterns in which *look* occurs are in some sense primary, thus requiring other (surface) syntactic patterns to be assimilated to them through some theoretical mechanism.[42]

Alongside the syntactic analysis, LG report a number of experiments that examine blind and sighted people's behavior to commands involving *look*. It is outside the scope of this research to review these experiments, but two conclusions LG come to are worth mentioning. The first is that, while for sighted people the meaning of *look* consists of a 'visual' component, for blind people the meaning seems to have instead a 'haptic' (i.e. relating to touch) component; and the second is that for both blind and sighted people the meaning of *look* centrally involves a component LG call 'exploratory'. As regards the first point, we believe that LG's conclusion is right and provides a good demonstration that the meaning of a form may be different for different people even within the same speech community, especially when real-world limitations (such as blindness) are involved.[43] As regards the second point, LG are led to posit 'exploratory' in the meaning because,

---

42.   In our analysis of *look*, no syntactically defined pattern is seen as primary in any way. We do consider, however, the visual uses of *look* to be, in a sense, primary in comparison to the purely intellectual usages (e.g., *look carefully at the problem*), and we have appealed to the mechanism of conceptual metaphor to explain such usages. The appeal to conceptual metaphor has been motivated on cognitive grounds, as explicated in Chapter 2.

43.   Another possibility (not explored further in this work) is hypothesizing the meaning of *look* to be ATTENTION, STRONGEST MODALITY rather than ATTENTION, VISUAL.

when given an object and told to look at it, the subjects in the experiment would seem to closely examine the object as opposed to merely glancing at it – in the case of the sighted subjects – or merely tapping it – in the case of the blind subjects. Note that our meaning of ATTENTION may explain this behavioral response equally well. Furthermore, our hypothesis – unlike EXPLORATORY – has explained large-scale distributional patterns that follow specifically from the notion of ATTENTION. For instance, the fact that *look* favors a preceding *but* in comparison to a preceding *and* has to do with the thematic importance of subsequent information in the text, as suggested both by the override effect of the use of *but* as well as by the use of the meaning ATTENTION. Similarly, the fact that *look* favors *at* in comparison to *on* or *in* has to do with the narrowing of the visual field, as suggested both by the use of the meaning ZERO-DIMENSIONAL LOCATION and again by the use of the meaning ATTENTION. It is difficult to see how EXPLORATORY could explain these and the other patterns noted in Chapters 3 and 4.

It will now be shown that (a) LG's componential analysis is filled with redundancy, positing in the meaning more than is necessary to account for the form's distribution; (b) their reliance on subcategorization frames leads them to misattribution, positing in the meaning elements that likely come from surrounding contextual features; and (c) their initial framing of the data in terms of the traditional a priori syntactic categories – that is, the fact that the object of study is the acquisition of *verbs* – limits the dataset and assumes in advance of analysis that there is more than one linguistic unit *look*.

First, then, seeing as the proposed meaning includes a component of 'visual' there is really no reason to posit in addition the component 'perceptual', because the notion of visual may by itself facilitate the inference of messages involving perception. LG have been led to 'perceptual' to differentiate *look* from *come* and *go* – other verbs that are posited to have 'motion' in their meaning, but 'visual' would have done the job equally well. Similarly, seeing as the meaning includes a component of 'exploratory' then there is no reason to posit in addition a component of 'activity', because the notion of exploratory by itself suggests messages involving activity. And again, if the meaning includes the components 'visual' and 'exploratory' then there is no reason to posit in addition to these the component 'inspection by eye', because the notions of visual and exploratory are together sufficient to lead speakers to the inference of messages involving inspection by eye. It is finally worth repeating that neither of the meaning components 'exploratory', 'activity' or 'inspection by eye' has lead LG to quantitative co-occurrence predictions of the type that the hypothesis of ATTENTION has been able to make.

Turning to the issue of misattribution, recall that the reason for positing 'motion' as a component in the meaning of *look* is its co-occurrence with locative prepositions (e.g., *look up*). But the notion of motion may well be contributed by the use of the locative itself (e.g., *up*) as well as other contextual features. If it were treated as a CS hypothesis, it would have to be shown that MOTION consistently contributes to the inference of message partials that are suggested by the use of *look* regardless of whether or not *look* co-occurs with forms that are indicative of location or direction. It is difficult to see, however, what MOTION might contribute in cases such as, say, *I like his new look* where no locative is present and where the intuition that one's gaze moves along a path seems quite irrelevant to the communicated message.

Finally, LG have biased their analysis by ignoring any occurrence of *look* where it is used with entity-suggesting morphology (e.g., *the look*). They further fail to address the issue that some of the meaning components they propose – such as 'activity' and 'exploratory' – are notions that straightforwardly contradict many of the common uses of *look*. The hypothesis proposed here has not restricted the dataset to cases where *look* co-occurs with verbal morphology and has consequently achieved a more comprehensive explanation of the distribution of *look*.

Before we turn to the next section, we may briefly mention the work of Levin (1993) who similarly offers a componential analysis of verb meaning. Levin argues that the semantic components that make up a verb determine the verb's syntactic behavior, particularly its expression of argument structure (1993: 10–11). Like LG, Levin posits several meaning components in *look* to accommodate its different syntactic behaviors. She classifies *look* as (a) a 'peer verb' (along with, e.g., *gape*) – a class of verbs characterized for taking a PP complement, typically *at*; (b) a 'stimulus subject perception verb' (along with, e.g., *smell*) – a class of verbs that take the stimulus as a subject and have an AdjP complement predicated of the stimulus (and a perceiver argument is optionally expressed in a PP); and (c) a 'rummage verb' (along with, e.g., *listen*) – a class of verbs that take two PP complements: the object being searched (typically with *for*), as well as the location (typically with *in*).

We agree with LG and Levin that regular patterns of co-occurrence of a given form follow from and may be indicative of the sign's (not verb) meaning. However, whereas Levin and LG can only point to correlations between the meaning components they propose and the syntactic patterns the form occurs in, we have been able to go beyond the correlation and offer an actual explanation of *why* a form with a certain meaning regularly appears in the environments that it does. For instance, Levin does nothing more than state that *look* regularly co-occurs with *at*, whereas we have explained why this is so. Indeed, we have explained at great length in Chapters 3 and 4 that *look* regularly co-occurs at greater than chance frequency with numerous other forms because its meaning, by hypothesis, contributes to the same aspect of the message as is contributed by the other form involved.

Note, further, that Levin characterizes the facts of the distribution of *look* in terms of abstract syntactic categories, such as PP – categories that are a priori with respect to the analysis of *look* – rather than in terms of units that are closer to the observation, such as *at*. The move to greater abstraction would be justified if it achieved greater explanatory power; but, in fact, our analysis of *look* has offered far more comprehensive and nuanced explanations of the distribution of *look*. For example, we have explained why *look* favors *at* in comparison to *on* or *in* despite the fact that all three sequences are found to occur, or why *look* – in comparison to *see* – disfavors the meaning LESS CONTROL, again, though both sequences occur. Finally, note that both LG and Levin derive the components in the meaning of *look* solely from an examination of patterns of co-occurrence that they already knew about prior to setting out to hypothesize what the meaning of *look* might be. Our meaning hypothesis, by contrast, has led us to the discovery of new distributional patterns, ones that were not known prior to the hypothesis.

## 3.   A construction analysis

Wierzbicka (1988) maintains that grammatical constructions are expressive devices that carry invariable meanings, and that the distribution of constructions is fully determined by their semantic values: "every grammatical construction is a vehicle of a certain semantic structure; and this is its *raison d'être*, and the criterion determining its range of use" (1988: 3). Replacing the term *grammatical construction* with *sign*, Wierzbicka's position appears quite aligned with our own. But there are at least two major differences. First, unlike our own approach, Wierzbicka's goal is not to *explain* the distribution of forms but rather to offer a semantic *description*: "we always keep in mind our main goal: an integrated semantic description of natural language" (1988: 3). Thus, meanings are not treated as hypotheses intended to explain distributions (both known and newly discovered), but rather the goal is to find the best description for distributional facts that are already known to the analyst in advance of the analysis. A corollary of this approach is that Wierzbicka fails to appeal to attested linguistic data as we have done, instead constructing decontextualized sentences and classifying some sentences as grammatical and others as ungrammatical. Wierzbicka's position further differs from ours in that she holds that individual lexical forms do not have meanings in isolation and receive meaning only when they occur within constructions: "the notion of the meaning of a word in isolation is in any case a fiction […] one cannot really say what a verb […] means, one can only say what a phrase […] means" (1988: 8). In other words,

Wierzbicka adopts a version of the compositional view of meaning,[44] and maintains that the meaning of a grammatical construction is primary while the meanings of the component parts of the construction are derived from, and receive their value only relative to, the meaning of the construction as a whole (1988: 9).[45]

Note that Wierzbicka is reluctant to agree that words have meaning in isolation because it appears to her that the meaning of an individual word changes from context to context. As explained at length in Chapter 1, this only seems to be the case when meaning is identified with the communicated message. Wierzbicka does believe, however, that grammatical constructions have stable invariant meanings. But below we will see that her proposed meaning of *have a look* fails to explain many of the attested uses of this putative construction.

Wierzbicka's analysis is of the putative construction *have a V*, in which *look* may figure (*have a look*).[46] To get at the meaning of the construction, Wierzbicka examines the differences between the uses of a verb generally and the uses of the same verb in the *have a V* construction. The first difference Wierzbicka notes is aspectual: the periphrastic construction presents the action as limited in time (1988: 297). Wierzbicka thus asserts that "one cannot say [...] ?*I had a long look*". Note now that had Wierzbicka examined attested data she would not have been able to make this statement. Indeed, there seems to be nothing incoherent about the example below.

(75)   I displaced a rock in Tennessee. Underneath, huddled at one edge of the exposed dirt, was a colony of ants. The slender ants moved slowly in the cool spring morning, and **I had a long look** at them before they vanished down their hole.                                   (*Natural History Magazine*)

Second, Wierzbicka maintains that the action reported by the *have a V* construction cannot have an external goal: it must be aimless, or aimed at some experience of the agent performing the action (1988: 298). Again, attested examples

---

44.   Unlike formal compositional approaches, Wierzbicka is quite explicit that the attempts to develop a semantics based on the notions of reference and truth have failed to be descriptively adequate. Rather than involving a relation between language and the world, Wierzbicka holds that meaning in natural language has more to do with how humans interpret the world: meaning is subjective and anthropocentric, reflecting cultural concerns and culture specific modes of interaction (1988: 2).

45.   One wonders why language users would bother to derive the meanings of words in a construction if they already had the meaning of the construction; and why would an analyst do it?

46.   Wierzbicka distinguishes between *have a V* and *have a N*, and for reasons not to be discussed here she classifies *look* in the former construction.

do not seem to corroborate this requirement. In the example below the action reported by *have a look* certainly seems to have an external goal: finding a present for Uncle Steve.

(76)   We're going to **have a look** for your Uncle Steve's birthday present.

*(Today's Parent)*

Third, Wierzbicka claims that the action must be seen as repeatable, something that can be done again and again. Actions which cannot be repeated cannot be described by the *have a V* construction (1988: 299). The problem here is that it is difficult to explicate what precisely makes an action repeatable, thus rendering this hypothesis unfalsifiable. For instance, Wierzbicka explains that one can *have a bite* because one can bite their sandwich again and again; yet, she continues, one cannot *have an eat* (this sequence marked as ungrammatical) because once one's sandwich has been eaten it cannot be eaten again. But, by the same token, we may say that once a bite has been bitten, *that* bite cannot be bitten again; or, after having eaten a sandwich, one *can* go on to eat another sandwich, and then another one. So, who is to say if an action can or cannot be seen as repeatable? At any rate, the repeatability of the action quite often seems to contribute nothing to the interpretation of texts where *have a look* occurs. Consider again Example (75), where the speaker *had a long look* at the ants until *they vanished down their hole*; there seems to be nothing in the communicated message that involves the repeatability of this action.

On the basis of these three criteria – action limited in time, no external goal and repeatability – Wierzbicka postulates the following semantic invariant: "The *have a V* construction is agentive, experiencer-oriented, antidurative, and reiterative" (1988: 300). But as our attested counterexamples demonstrate, this semantic invariant appears to be at odds with the facts.

Now Wierzbicka continues to explain that her tentative meaning would wrongly predict that people should also say things like *have a kneel-down*, which she marks as ungrammatical. This data leads her to add another semantic component to her posited meaning to the effect that the *have a V* construction implies that the activity is enjoyable, pleasurable or potentially good for the agent (1988: 301). *Have a kneel-down* is then ruled out because, Wierzbicka maintains, it is not seen as an enjoyable action. But then, Wierzbicka acknowledges, this additional component in the meaning seems to be at odds with the possibility of utterances such as *It's awful – just have a look at it!* where the possibility of an enjoyable effect is certainly not implied. Such data motivates Wierzbicka to classify perception verbs (e.g., *look*, *taste*, etc.) as a special subtype of the *have a V* construction. And this subtype has the additional meaning of an action "which could cause one to find out (to come to know) something about something" (1988: 302). Still, this is argued to be a subtype of the general *have a V* construction because even here, Wierzbicka argues, the action implies a beneficial (even if not enjoyable) effect "since obtaining knowledge would be generally described as something good rather than bad" (1988: 302). Note that here Wierzbicka posits a semantic description which depends on the analyst's personal views on the value of knowledge. But even conceding that point, there seems to be cases where no beneficial effect to the agent is implied.

(77)  Hate to be a pain but could you maybe just **have a quick look** in these files to see if they are correct please?
(http://modthesims.info/d/archive/index.php?t-505906.html)

In this example, the speaker seems to imply quite the opposite of a "potential mental gain" (1988: 306) to the agent, as suggested by *hate to be a pain but could you maybe just... please*; indeed, the purpose of the action here is entirely for the benefit of the person making the request and not at all for the benefit of the person performing the action. This example then again serves to falsify Wierzbicka's claim that the *have a V* construction cannot be used when the goal of performing the action is external to the agent.

Finally, Wierzbicka claims that the perception-verb subtype of the *Have a V* construction adds to the meaning of the verb the idea of a half-hearted, casual, and not totally serious effort: "the expression *have a look at* seems to suggest a lack of zeal and commitment" (1988: 306). Yet again, attested examples seem to falsify this proposed semantic component.

(78)  We need to **have a long, hard, serious look** at airport departure tax—and I know the Chancellor would have a cardiac arrest but the sums stack up.
(http://www.parliament.the-stationery-office.co.uk/pa/cm200405/
cmselect/cmniaf/53/5030110.htm)

In sum, the main problem with Wierzbicka's analysis is that she tries to identify the meaning of the construction exclusively on the basis of introspectively-derived data (i.e., constructed sentences judged for grammaticality) rather than objectively observable facts of actual language use. Once attested examples are examined, each and every one of the meaning components she proposes for *have a look* is falsified. Notice, further, that Wierzbicka's analysis cannot make predictions of the sort we have been making. For example, in Chapter 1 we demonstrated that *look* favors *careful* in comparison to *first*. There does not appear to be anything in Wierzbicka's analysis that could lead to this prediction. In fact, her claim that the *have a look* construction has a meaning component involving a casual action would seem to predict that *careful* should actually *not* be favored. Lastly, Wierzbicka offers no explanation of the well-known fact that *have a look*, much like *look* in isolation, favors *at* in comparison to *on* or *in* despite all three sequences occurring in texts. This piece of data was not shown in Chapter 3, and so we offer it here now.

**Table 67.** COCA searches for *at*, *on* and *in* (for *have a look*)

|  | Sequence | Tokens |
|---|---|---|
| Favored | *[have] a look at* | 486 |
| Disfavored | *[have] a look on* | 24 |
|  | *[have] a look in* | 21 |

**Table 68.** Total COCA occurrences of *at*, *on* and *in* in the presence and absence of *have a look*

|  | *have a look* present | | *have a look* absent | |
|---|---|---|---|---|
|  | N | % | N | % |
| *at* | 486 | 91 | 2265757 | 16 |
| *on* | 24 | 5 | 3134810 | 23 |
| *in* | 21 | 4 | 8363166 | 61 |
| Total | 531 | 100 | 13763733 | 100 |

The hypothesis of ATTENTION, VISUAL explains this data much as it explains the favoring by *look* for *at* when *have* is absent; positing *have a look* as a construction does not add here any explanatory strength.

   To conclude thus far, unlike LG, Levin and Wierzbicka, our hypothesis has resulted from an unbiased and unrestricted dataset and has therefore made it possible to posit a single *look* with one invariant meaning that, as has been demonstrated throughout this book, can successfully explain all occurrences of this form in spoken and written texts. Also unlike LG, Levin and Wierzbicka, our analysis has allowed us to go beyond the facts of co-occurrence that were known to the analysts prior to their analyses and actually explain *why* these patterns of co-occurrence are as they are. Indeed, our research is the only one that has led to the discovery of numerous patterns of co-occurrence that were not known prior to the meaning hypotheses proposed in this work.

## 4.   A markedness analysis

Turning finally to Tobin (1993) who has a similar goal to that of the analysis proposed here, that is, to explain speakers' expressive choices of *look* and of *see*. According to Tobin's hypothesis, *look* and *see* share the meaning VISUAL; the two signs differ, however, due to a semantic parameter called RESULT, for which *see* is claimed to be *marked* and *look* is claimed to be neutral or, *unmarked* (1993: 63–5). Accordingly, *see* expresses a visual action, state or event that is specifically seen from the point of view of its RESULT, which involves the reception of visual sensory input (e.g., *He saw the picture*); *look*, by contrast, expresses a visual action state or event which may or may not involve a RESULT (e.g., *He looked at the picture* involving a result, versus *He looked but saw nothing* not involving a result).

By giving *look* the unmarked meaning, Tobin intends to explain why *look* is used much more diversely than *see*, e.g., in all of *He looked at me, He looked blankly, He looked but didn't see, He looks happy, his new look*, etc. These utterances all communicate message elements involving VISUAL yet none, it is argued, is specifically seen from the point of view of RESULT, and some do not involve RESULT at all. On the other hand, by Tobin's hypothesis, the notion of RESULT is always contributed by the use of *see*, even if the visual stimulus is only implicit. For example, the meaning RESULT explains the use of *see* in *I see well with these glasses* because the message involves the reception of visual sensory input in a particular manner.

While Tobin appeals to the unmarked status of the meaning of *look* to explain the more diverse distribution of this form, its unmarked status alone is incapable of explaining on what basis speakers choose *look* over *see* when 'result' *is* a feature of the message being communicated. For example, why do speakers sometimes say *look at it* and sometimes *see it* if both utterances may communicate a message partial involving the reception of visual sensory input? To account for the distribution of *look*, therefore, Tobin also defines the unmarked status of *look* in positive terms, explaining that being unmarked for RESULT amounts to having the meaning PROCESS.[47] Thus, his hypothesized meaning of *look* may be rendered VISUAL PROCESS. By this hypothesis, the reason speakers would choose *look* as opposed to *see* in, say, *look at it* is that they want to contribute specifically to a message partial involving visual process. But, if *look* invariably contributes the semantic notion of PROCESS, as Tobin's analysis clearly intends to demonstrate (see the micro-level analysis on pp. 65–70), then what does the hypothesis of its unmarked status add to the explanation? In other words, if the explanation anyway must always appeal

---

47.   Tobin initially states that when the unmarked form *look* is used then the visual action "may be viewed either from the point of view of a PROCESS *and/or* a RESULT" (1993: 63–4; emphasis, N.S), implying that *look* does not necessarily contribute to a message feature of 'process'. But then, if *look* can contribute to a message feature of 'result' while *not* contributing to a message feature of 'process' then it is difficult to explain why speakers would ever choose *look* as opposed to *see*. And indeed, in the course of actual analyses, Tobin repeatedly appeals to the notion of 'process' in explaining why *look* occurs where it does.

to the notion of PROCESS, then why not make the simpler claim – the one that avoids the a priori postulation of a markedness category in the grammar – and just hypothesize VISUAL PROCESS as the meaning of *look*?[48]

Now VISUAL PROCESS seems a rather unconvincing explanation for why speakers choose *look* over *see*. For example, it is not quite clear that the notion of PROCESS plays a role in utterances such as *You look beautiful*. Tobin explains the use of *look* in such cases as follows: "these examples describe a process of *how* someone or something [...] is developing and progressing as it is being observed, usually at the time of encoding" (1993: 65, emphasis in original). But a different interpretation of these utterances may be that the message actually concerns the result, not the process, of the visual event because it is precisely the reception of visual sensory input that enables one to make the judgment or attribution communicated through these utterances. Unlike our own analysis of *look beautiful* (Example 12 in Chapter 2), Tobin's analysis relies on his own subjective interpretation, without appealing to independent linguistic evidence in the texts where *look* occurs.

Consider now why ATTENTION provides a better explanation than PROCESS for the choice of *look*. For one, PROCESS cannot explain why *look* is used in examples such as the following, repeated here from Chapter 3.

(79)   She stood holding the calendar forward between the tips of her fingers, as if she were a photograph with the focus on the calendar and her own figure blurred in its background. [...] "Would you like to **look** at this calendar, Peter?"                                                                    (*The Fountainhead*)

In Example (79) Peter certainly needs to visually register the calendar to answer to Dominique's request. Tobin's hypothesis would have a hard time explaining why *look* has been chosen here rather than *see* (e.g. why not *Would you like to see this calendar, Peter?*). But our hypothesis has a straightforward answer: *look* is chosen because Dominique wants Peter to *attend* to the calendar, as is independently evident in the text in the use of, e.g., *focus on the calendar* or *this*.

Finally, the hypothesis of PROCESS cannot lead the analyst to discover – much less explain – the quantitative distributional facts that have been noted in this manuscript. With respect to the example above, unlike ATTENTION, PROCESS cannot explain why *look* favors co-occurrence with *this* in comparison to *the*; this favoring has nothing to do with the notion of process but it straightforwardly follows from the hypothesis of ATTENTION. Likewise, PROCESS will not be able to

---

48. It may be noted that such a hypothesis would not preclude the reception of visual sensory input from being a feature of the communicated message; only this feature would be an inference following from the meaning PROCESS as well as other contextual clues which may be present.

explain why *look* favors a preceding *but* in comparison to a preceding *and*, or why it favors *carefully* in comparison to *carelessly*, or even why *look* favors *at* in comparison to *on* and *in*. Similarly, the hypotheses of PROCESS and RESULT for *look* and *see*, respectively, cannot explain why *look* – in comparison to *see* – favors *this*, or why *look* favors *but*, or why *look* favors *notice*. Yet all these favorings and more have been explained in terms of the meaning hypotheses proposed here.

# CHAPTER 6

# Theoretical excursus

## A critique of William Diver's approach to the grammar-lexicon divide and a recapitulation of analytical assumptions and findings

## 1. Introduction

In his thinking about the place of meaning in linguistic theory, William Diver was always careful to begin linguistic analyses without framing the observations in terms of the a priori syntactic categories of sentence grammar. But the a priori classification of some linguistic forms as grammatical and of others as lexical nonetheless remained a feature of Diver's thinking, much as it has for nearly all linguists. The distinction between grammar and lexicon captures an impressionistic difference that the meanings of some linguistic forms seem open to introspection (e.g., *cat*) whereas the meanings of others are not (e.g., *the*). Other seemingly observational differences are that grammatical forms, in comparison to lexical forms, tend to be smaller units; tend to occur more frequently in texts; and tend to occur as affixes, or satellites, to lexical forms. But above all, the reason why this a priori distinction was sustained in the thinking of Diver and has continued in others in CS is the fact that – unlike the admittance of the traditional grammatical categories (noun, verb, etc.) – the assumption of a grammar and a lexicon had seemed (if only implicitly) analytically harmless; indeed, the classification of a form as grammatical (as opposed to lexical) has never hindered a successful invariant meaning hypothesis. Yet despite this perceived harmlessness, the assumptions that have been associated with a grammar-lexicon classification – primarily, the assumption that invariant meanings are the province of grammar alone – have come with a price. These assumptions, as we shall see in the next section, were all made a priori and, in light of the apparent strength of the hypotheses of the present study, prove rather misguided. The present work has endeavored to demonstrate that an invariant meaning hypothesis can succeed quite well in explaining speakers' choice of a lexical form; all that was necessary was to let go of the a priori assumptions regarding the nature of the lexicon, and instead proceed to test lexical meaning hypotheses by the same exact analytical principles that have normally been applied to grammar.

Section 2 elaborates the above discussion concerning the differential status of the categories of grammar and lexicon in CS. Then, Section 3 will conclude this manuscript with some recapitulations of the major findings and contributions of the present work.

## 2.   The linguistic status of the categories of grammar and lexicon

Diver (2012: Section 4, 1995 [2012]: Section 3.2.1.4) maintains that grammar and lexicon constitute two different types of hypothesis; the essential difference among them involves "the way that the meanings in a list relate to each other". Lexical meanings constitute an open-ended list where each meaning stands independent of the meaning of any other form; for example, the meaning of *cat* could be stated without recourse to the meaning of *dog*, or even of *animal* (though the meanings may well share some semantic content, as has been proposed here for *look* and *see*). Grammatical meanings, by contrast, cluster in closed lists – systems – where meanings stand in a relation of closed opposition to one another and thus mutually define one another;[49] for example, the statement of the meaning of *that* – LESS DEIXIS – depends for its interpretation and testing on its opposition to the meaning of *this* – MORE DEIXIS. In short, a sign is grammatical if its meaning is systemic, and is lexical if its meaning is independent. I would like to propose here that this ought to be recognized as *the sole* basis for distinguishing between grammar and lexicon, because this is the only criterion that allows for the distinction between grammar and lexicon to emerge from an analytical procedure that itself is neutral to the distinction.[50]

---

49.   The meanings in a system also typically exhaust the relevant semantic substance.

50.   In keeping with the CS methodological principle of beginning analysis with the smallest possible problem, the analyst ought to begin with just one potential signal and attempt to formulate a meaning that accounts for its distribution. If the analysis succeeds then we have an independent – that is, lexical – meaning hypothesis. But the analysis might fail, and the reason may be that the deployment of the putative sign, call it sign A, is influenced by the availability of signs B and C whose meanings offer speakers competing expressive alternatives. The consequence is that sign A is absent in places where its hypothesis would lead one to expect it. In this case, the analyst must explore the distributions of signs B and C and posit tentative meaning hypotheses that would explain why the distributions of each sign differ (in Chapter 4 we have explored the constraining effect of *see*, *seem* and *appear* on the distribution of *look*). If that analysis succeeds then we still have only independent – lexical – meaning hypotheses. But, it may be that in the course of exploring the different distributions of signs A, B and C, the analyst finds that one cannot formulate a substantive meaning of A that makes

Other assumptions that have been associated with the categories of grammar and lexicon are all a priori and prove unwarranted in light of the results of the present research. These other assumptions (all summarized in *The Grammar of Modern English – a Columbia School Primer*, an unpublished manuscript by Alan Huffman) are: (a) that grammar and lexicon form a continuum; (b) that invariant meanings are the province of grammar whereas in the lexicon there is polysemy; (c) that due to their lack of systemic opposition, lexical meanings do not constrain the choice of one another as do grammatical meanings; and finally (d) that grammatical distinctions are imposed by the language whereas lexical distinctions are imposed by real world categorizations.[51] In each of the next subsections we examine these points in detail and see why they are at odds with other tenets of CS linguistics.

## 2.1 The a priori assumption of a grammar-lexicon continuum

The idea of a grammar-lexicon continuum has not (explicitly, at least) originated in the thinking of Diver; rather, it is a familiar idea that seems to have made its way to CS through the work of cognitive linguists (see Huffman 2012: 17). Cognitivists, in turn, have come to posit a continuum in response to generative theory where grammar and lexicon are qualitatively seen as two completely different types of entities in the linguistic system: for the generativists, the term grammar applies to a set of innate principles that exist independent of the communicative function of language and that underlie one's linguistic knowledge; the lexicon, by contrast, is seen as a kind of dictionary, a list of idiosyncrasies that must be learned through exposure, and which in turn allows speakers to put the innate grammatical knowledge into operation (see, e.g., Haegeman 1994: 16). In direct contrast to the view of the generativists, cognitive linguists make the initial assumption that language is first and foremost an instrument of communication and consequently, that linguistic constructs – whether lexical or grammatical – are all inherently symbolic: "lexicon, morphology and syntax make up a continuum consisting solely of *assemblies of symbolic structures*" (Langacker 2004: 21, original emphasis). This is then the form of the continuum. At the lexicon end there are particular

---

clear how it differs from B or C. In that case, the only way the analyst can differentiate them is to define A as *not* – one way or another – being the other/s. When such meanings are posited a CS grammatical system has been created (Reid, personal communication).

51.  Of course, there have been successful CS hypotheses – such as Crupi's (2004) hypothesis for *yet*, *but* and *still* – of independent meanings that are nonetheless invariant, constrain the deployment of one another, and offer a linguistically-imposed categorization. One might think that these forms that Crupi studied fall somewhere in the middle on the grammar-lexicon continuum. But this is untenable, as will be explained.

concrete words or constructions, such as *I, I don't* or *I am*. At the grammar end there are purely schematic constructions, that is, abstract patterns of symbolization, such as SVO, that emerge from the frequency of use of particular complex expressions (e.g., *I ate the cookie, She saw mom*, etc.). And lastly, in the middle of the continuum there are various different types of constructions that are partly schematic and partly concrete, such as *the more X the more Y* (e.g., *the more you study the more you'll know*).

Note now that given the CS conception of grammar – which is quite different from the cognitivist conception delineated above – a grammar-lexicon continuum becomes, upon inspection, simply untenable. First, unlike cognitive linguists, an appeal to the degree of how schematic or how concrete a linguistic unit is plays absolutely no role in CS in the identification of a linguistic unit as grammatical or lexical; indeed, the schemas posited by cognitive grammars typically involve a priori syntactic categories which, for the most part, CS analysts do without. Instead, as explicated above, in CS the term grammar has been applied to meanings that constitute a closed system, whereas the term lexicon has been applied to forms whose semantic value is independent. Now, whereas cognitive analyses can permit linguistic units that are partly schematic partly concrete, a CS analysis could never permit a linguistic unit that is partly systemic, partly independent; the meaning of a particular sign is either hypothesized to be a part of a system or it is not. Indeed, despite talking of a grammar-lexicon continuum, no CS analysis has ever proposed that a hypothesized sign actually stands in the middle.

Nonetheless, Huffman (2012: 17) informally cites prepositions and adverbs as forms that may occupy the middle of the putative continuum. But in the analytical history of CS, whenever forms traditionally classified as prepositions or adverbs were studied, the result always involved either a systemic or an independent meaning hypothesis. For example, Reid (2004) offers a systemic meaning hypothesis for the forms *at, on* and *in* (even though he, too, talks of these forms in various places as if they were lexical, e.g., on p. 105). But, because Reid's hypothesis involves a closed system where the meanings in the system are mutually defined, these forms should be recognized as 100 percent grammatical; (it may sometimes be forgotten that their traditional classification as prepositions need have no bearing on their status). On the other hand, Crupi (2004) offers an analysis of the forms *yet, but* and *still* and posits an independent meaning hypothesis for each; hence, *yet, but* and *still* should be recognized as 100 percent lexical.

## 2.2 The a priori assumption of polysemy in the lexicon

As discussed extensively in Chapter 1, Diver's principled distinction between the linguistically encoded meaning on the one hand and the subjective experience of message partials on the other is what makes the hypothesis of an invariant meaning feasible; yet it seems Diver only applied the meaning-message distinction to grammar while uncritically continuing to accept unrestricted polysemy in the lexicon, so much so as to resist applying the technical term *meaning* altogether to lexical units (see Diver 1995 [2012]: Section 3.3.2; Huffman 2012: 17; Reid 2004: 122). Reid (2004: 105) notes that Diver was particularly apprehensive that an uncontrolled appeal to metaphor would allow a lexical analysis to escape falsification.[52] While our analysis has appealed to metaphor to explain some of the uses of *look*, the justification for and status of conceptual metaphor vis-à-vis our hypothesis were carefully controlled. Various pieces of empirical evidence independent of the use of *look* were brought forth in support of the conceptual link between vision and intellection. And, it is precisely the recognition that this conceptual link is a feature of cognition generally rather than of language particularly that has freed our analysis from the need to evoke polysemy in the linguistic code. Rather than identifying non-visual interpretations as an additional meaning of *look*, our analysis has treated the metaphor as merely another way that the hypothesized meaning can contribute to the communication of the ongoing message.

Note, further, that the assumption that invariant meanings are the province of grammar alone is inconsistent with the CS view that a language is an inventory of signs. As explicated in Chapter 1, the identification of a sign only follows a successful joint-hypothesis of a signal corresponding to an invariant meaning. But, if there are forms in the language that are lexical and therefore lack – by definition – invariant meanings, how could these forms ever be identified by a CS analysis as signs? In other words, Diver's views regarding polysemy in the lexicon defy the possibility of a lexical *hypothesis* (though, as mentioned above, Diver did talk of the lexicon as a hypothesis); at best, it can offer a description, much as would a dictionary. And finally, the notion of a grammar-lexicon continuum fails again, this time because a meaning hypothesis cannot be partly invariant, partly polysemous;[53] partly polysemous is polysemous, and polysemous senses cannot

---

52. One wonders why this apprehension – which in general terms concerns the problem of polysemy – was not handled by the same analytical principles that have guided Diver's thinking on grammar – where the risk of polysemy is no less.

53. The possibility of a form being in the middle of the continuum for being fully systemic (like grammar) and yet polysemous (like lexicon) is also impossible to sustain as a CS hypothesis, because CS cannot admit of polysemy (see Reid 2004). The alternative – a form that is fully independent (like lexicon) and fully invariant (like grammar, according to Diver) – is precisely what we have proposed in this book for *look*. But no one wants to argue that *look* is in the middle of the continuum.

be sustained as a CS hypothesis (see arguments in Chapter 2: Sections 1 and 7, as well as discussion in Reid 2004: Section 9).

## 2.3   The a priori assumption that only grammatical forms constrain one another

There is no doubt that the meanings of a grammatical system constrain the deployment of one another, yet there is every reason to believe that the meanings of lexical units do so, too. Still, one argument Diver offered for this supposed differential status of grammar and lexicon involves a thought experiment speculating on what might happen if some form were to suddenly drop out of the language (see, e.g., Diver 1995 [2012]: Section 3.2.1.4). If it were a grammatical form that dropped out of usage then the consequence would necessarily be a reshuffling of the other meanings in the system, influencing of course their deployment by speakers. This is so because grammatical meanings are only understood via their value relative to other grammatical meanings in the same system; thus, any alteration in one part of the system shifts the value of the other members. By contrast, if a lexical form were to suddenly drop out of usage then this, Diver maintains, need not have consequences for any other form in the language. Now this may seem true with respect to forms like *cat* or *deer* – Diver's examples. But, as we have seen in the analyses of Chapter 4, a speaker's choice of the hypothesized sign *look* is certainly influenced by the availability of the signs *see*, *seem* and *appear*, whose meanings offer speakers competing expressive alternatives despite not forming a closed system. Indeed, *look* sometimes fails to occur in places where its hypothesized meaning might lead one to expect it to occur (e.g., in *Objects in mirror are closer than they* **appear**). The explanation for its occasional absence has been offered in terms of the constraining effect of the hypothesized meanings of *see*, *seem* and *appear* on the distribution of *look*. Returning now to Diver's thought experiment, if somehow, say, *appear* were to drop out of the language, it may well be that the distribution (and eventually meaning) of *look* would change accordingly so as to cover some of the area where previously speakers were choosing *appear*; (for example, in the hypothetical absence of *appear*, *Objects in mirror are closer than they* **look** might turn out to be the best way to express the intended message).

## 2.4   The a priori assumption that lexical meanings are based on real-world categorizations

Given the fact that Diver most emphatically adopted Saussure's assertion that "language is a principle of classification" (Diver 1974 [2012]: 31), it is ironic that Huffman states that lexical meanings reflect real-world categorizations rather than being imposed by the language. Saussure is here making the point that a language may divide up a spectrum of conceptual possibilities any way it likes and that the conceptual distinctions languages make are, therefore, arbitrary. Interestingly, while Diver adopted this truism wholeheartedly to grammar, Saussure's own examples come from the domain of lexicon. For instance, Saussure notes that English distinguishes *river* and *stream* on the basis of size whereas French distinguishes *riviere* and *fleuve* on the basis of whether the water flows into the sea (see Culler 1976: 33–4). Similarly, in our own analysis of *look* and *see* it would be difficult to maintain that the hypothesized difference between them – ATTENTION versus EXPERIENCING – amounts to a straightforward real-world categorization. There are conceivably other ways that the semantic domain of vision could have been partitioned and it is quite probable that different languages draw somewhat different distinctions. For example, out of context, *look* would be translated to Hebrew as *histakel* while *see* would be translated as *ra'a*. But, to take just one type of a seemingly unusual case, in many imperative contexts where English speakers use *look* (such as, say, in *Hey, come look at this bird!*), Hebrew speakers use *ra'a* (*Hey, bo tire'e et ha-zipor ha-zot*). Of course a full analysis would be required, but it does seem that the (as yet unknown) meanings of the visual forms in Hebrew do not match precisely the hypothesized meanings of *look* and *see* in English. It seems therefore that, despite the lexical status of the forms involved, each language nonetheless imposes its own distinctions on the semantic domain of vision (see also Otheguy 1995: 218).

## 2.5   Conclusion

The assumptions we have examined regarding the nature of the lexicon have served in the history of CS to bias the selection of forms of interest for analysis: from its inception, the choice of CS linguists has been to concentrate on grammatical forms since, as we have seen, the a priori assumptions made about lexicon and grammar have rendered lexical analysis impossible to execute.[54] But the choice to concentrate on grammatical forms has also been justified as follows: "a premature stab at lexical analysis might risk misattributing to lexicon what properly belongs to grammar" (Huffman 2012: 17). In our own case, for example, resting on the shoulders of successful CS hypotheses of grammatical formatives, we have appealed to the presence of entity- and event-suggesting morphologies (such as *the* or *-ed*), thus freeing us from the need to attribute these message

---

54.   Reid (1991) presents some lexical analyses (e.g. *person* and *people*, *wheat* and *oat*, *fruit* and *vegetable*, etc.), though none is fully worked out, and all are brought forth in service of the analysis of the grammatical system of Entity Number.

partials to the meaning of *look*. Indeed, Huffman proposes that understanding the contribution of grammar to communication would help to elucidate what the contribution of lexicon might be (2012: 17). So now, after a great many successful grammatical hypotheses offered in the CS framework, the time has finally come to recognize that the potential risk of misattribution has significantly diminished, and that the contribution of lexicon can safely be explored. Our analysis has shown that the CS term *meaning* can apply to lexicon in precisely the same way as it has previously applied to grammar. The biases and assumptions CS analysts have long held about the lexicon have proved wrong for *look*, a word all agree is lexical. Indeed, in our analysis of *look* we have discovered that no reason to evoke polysemy actually arises, much as this has been discovered time and again for grammatical forms. All the rationales and testing techniques used by CS analysts in validating meaning hypotheses of grammatical systems have proven here equally applicable.

## 3.   Recapitulations

This work has posited a meaning hypothesis for *look* that has explained the distribution of that form in documented acts of speaking and writing; furthermore, the hypothesis has given rise to numerous genuine predictions (that is, predictions to hitherto unknown facts) of quantitative co-occurrence favorings that have been confirmed in a massive corpus of English texts produced by thousands of speakers. In addition to doing what all scientific predictions do, namely increasing our confidence in the hypothesis that produced them, the predictions made here provide us with new knowledge about the distribution of *look, see* and other forms that may provide useful for other scholars.

The qualitative analyses have explicated the fit of the hypothesized meaning – ATTENTION, VISUAL – with the various different types of messages or message partials suggested by the use of *look*. For example, the hypothesized meaning has explained why speakers choose *look* for the communication of message partials involving visual activity (e.g., *looked carefully at the photo*), message partials involving attribution (e.g., *look beautiful*), and message partials involving visual features (e.g., *rely on my looks*). In all of these cases, *look* is chosen because visual attention is a feature of the communicated message. The characteristics of the message that are relevant to the validation of the meaning hypothesis have not been the product of the analyst's intuition or knowledge of English, but have been consistently demonstrated through the independent presence of particular forms available in the attested texts whose communicative effects partially overlap with that of *look*. In explaining the choice to utter *look*, we have also endeavored to explain why other closely related forms, such as *see* and *appear*, were not chosen in the contexts under study.

As part of the analysis, we have seen that the meaning of *look* underdetermines the messages it can be used to communicate. Indeed, it is this gap between meaning and message that has enabled a single invariant meaning to explain by itself all occurrences of *look* without the need to invoke either polysemy or homonymy. We have thus had no need to posit a '*look*-verb and a '*look*-noun', recognizing that the message partials involving an act of visually attending as opposed to visual features are attributable to the surrounding morphology (such as *-ed* or *the*). More generally, we have attempted to show that the classification into lexical form classes is not equipped to explain, nor discover, the many peculiarities in the distribution of *look* that we have discovered and explained. The syntactic classification can at best explain why, say, *look* co-occurs with *-ed* (because it is a verb, it would be said), but it cannot explain – as we have done – why, for instance, *look* co-occurs with *this* at a higher than chance frequency in comparison to *the*; or why – on a particular occasion – *look* is chosen as opposed to *see*; or why – on a particular occasion – *look* is chosen as opposed to *appearance*.

In order to explain facts of this sort an appeal to the meaning of the form is required. In speculating about the meaning of *look*, previous studies have nonetheless let the traditional syntactic categories guide the semantic analysis. Thus, Gruber (1967), Landau and Gleitman (1985), Levin (1993) and others have all restricted their dataset only to verbal uses of *look* and, in order to explain how its distribution differs from *see*, have posited a feature of 'activity' in the meaning of *look*. But 'activity' contradicts uses such as found in *the new look* or *looking good*, where no activity seems to be at issue. These analysts have thus been led to positing more than one linguistic unit *look* (a verb and a noun, at least) – inevitably, because the analysis began from a biased dataset that completely left out many of the different uses of this form. The hypothesis proposed here, by contrast, has made no a priori assumptions about lexical form classes, and has treated every occurrence of *look* as equally the responsibility of the hypothesis. Looking at an unbiased and unrestricted dataset, a unified explanation for the full range of the distribution of *look* has become feasible and, as in the case of the present work, has enabled the generation of supporting verifiable predictions.

Furthermore, much as we saw no need to posit '*look*-verb' and '*look*-noun', we also saw no need to posit constructions that exist as linguistic units over and above their component parts. Instead, the message partials that are often communicated through frequent sequences such as *look for* (search), *look up to* (admire), *look after* (take care of), etc. have been explained in terms of the contribution of the hypothesized meaning of *look* – together with the contribution of the forms it co-occurs with.[55] Indeed, the hypothesized meaning ATTENTION, VISUAL has explained why *look* is chosen even when, say, *look up to* is used for a communication that does *not* involve a message of admiration. The meanings of the putative constructions thus empirically fail as explanatory hypotheses for the distributions of these sequences because these sequences are sometimes used for the communication of message partials that are quite different from the ones proposed as the meanings of these constructions.

We have further had no reason to posit two senses of *look* – one 'visual' and another 'intellectual'. Nonetheless, like the cognitivists, we have appealed to the conceptual metaphor mapping the domain of vision to the domain of intellection to explain uses of *look* such as found in *look at how you're thinking*. But, unlike the cognitivists, we have concluded that there is no need to build the metaphor into the linguistic code. It is precisely because the conceptual link is a feature of cognition generally rather than of language specifically that VISUAL alone is sufficient to explain both the visual and intellectual messages. Moreover, the hypothesis of separate visual and intellectual senses is impossible to falsify because there are many occurrences where the two putative senses are combined and blend into one another. If the analyst only considers a handful of examples, some like *look at the photo* and others like *look at how you're thinking*, then it may well appear that the uses of *look* fall neatly into discrete conceptual categories, one involving only vision and another involving only intellection. But as more examples are analyzed, the conceptual space between the putative senses fills in, revealing a continuum that defies a principled partitioning. We have seen numerous examples where the communicated message simultaneously involves both vision and intellection, thus only lending further support to the conceptual metaphor being a general feature of cognition, and obviating the need of positing 'intellectual' as a secondary sense.

The classification of *look* into lexical form classes, as well as the positing of constructions of which *look* is only a part, and the positing of visual and intellectual senses – all result from an underlying assumption (one that is set aside here) that the meanings of linguistic forms are available to introspection, and can be known to the analyst simply by virtue of the subjective experience of understanding communicative intents in utterances. In other words, many linguists are accustomed to identifying the meaning of a form with some aspect of the message

---

55.   While there are no fully worked out hypotheses for the meanings of the other forms in these sequences, the postulated meaning of *look* nonetheless survives in these combinations, as has been shown through the presence of contextual evidence indicating that visual attention is a feature of the communicated message wherever *look* occurs.

communicated on a particular occasion of the form's use. It thus may seem that a component in the meaning of *look* is 'activity' because the message communicated on some occasions of its use involves an element of activity; or it may seem that the meaning of *look up to* is 'admire' because the message communicated on some occasions involves a message partial of admiring. When the meaning of a form is thus identified with the conceptual fractions of message or message partials that the form is involved in, the analyst is inevitably led to positing multiple linguistic units per form because virtually all forms are used for the communication of many different types of messages or message partials.

The success of the meaning hypothesis proposed here in explaining the distribution of *look* has crucially depended on William Diver's fundamental distinction between, on the one hand, the invariant meaning – that which is a part of the linguistic code – and, on the other, the message or message partial – the interpretation of the code through a process of inference. Rather than encoding messages, meanings are here seen as merely sparse notional fragments that provide but hints, prompts from which many different types of message elements can be inferred. While the hypothesized semantic value of *look* is sparse, it has been shown to provide precisely the right amount of semantic substance that is necessary to explain all of its different uses, as well as to explain why *look* is chosen where *see*, *seem* and *appear* may initially appear as plausible alternatives.

Turning now to a recapitulation of some of the quantitative data. As noted, the hypothesized meaning has been empirically supported through large scale quantitative predictions testing for the regular co-occurrence of *look* with particular other forms that, by hypothesis, are chosen by speakers to produce partially overlapping message effects. For example, the hypothesized meaning we have abbreviated as ATTENTION, VISUAL has explained why *look* co-occurs with *carefully* at a higher than chance frequency in comparison to *carelessly*. Previous analyses, as mentioned above, have all classified *look* as an activity verb and have used this classification to explain why *look* – but not *see* – co-occurs with *carefully*. But *carefully* and *carelessly* are equally applicable modifications for activities and both modifications are found to co-occur with *look*. Our hypothesis is, as far as one can tell, the only one that could explain why it is that *look* favors *carefully* in particular (noting that this favoring is particular to *look* and does not extend to just any form that is used to denote an activity). Furthermore, the hypothesized meaning has explained why *look* co-occurs with *at* at a higher than chance frequency in comparison to *on* and *in*. Of course, everyone already knew that *look at* is most frequent but our hypothesis (together with Reid's 2004 hypotheses of the meanings of *at*, *on* and *in*) has explained *why* this is so: it is (in a nutshell) because *look* and *at* – each due to its hypothesized meaning – both contribute to a message feature involving a narrowing of the visual field.

In addition to these patterns of distribution that may have long been known, the hypothesized meaning has also led to the discovery of numerous peculiarities in the distribution of *look* that have been noted here, and explained, for the first time. For example, the hypothesis of ATTENTION has led to the discovery that *look* co-occurs with *this* at a higher than chance frequency in comparison to *the*. Or again, our hypothesis has discovered and explained why *look* co-occurs with a preceding *but* at a higher than chance frequency in comparison to a preceding *and*. Moreover, the hypotheses of both *look* and *see* have also explained why *look* favors co-occurrence with *this* more so than *see*, and again, why *look* favors co-occurrence with a preceding *but* more so than *see*.

Furthermore, by positing meaning hypotheses for *see, seem* and *appear* we have explained why *look* is sometimes absent where its hypothesis might lead the analyst to expect it. For example, the hypothesized meaning of *see* – EXPERIENCING VISUALLY – has explained why *see* favors co-occurrence with a following *a* more so than *look*; the hypothesis for *appear* – INITIATION OF PERCEPTION – has explained why *appear* favors co-occurrence with a following *but* more so than *look*; and lastly, the hypothesis for *seem* – PERSPECTIVE DEPENDENCY – has explained why *seem* favors co-occurrence with *at the time* more so than *look*. These are all newly discovered distributional facts that have only just been revealed through our meaning hypotheses.

It is worth mentioning that the hypothesized meanings of *look* and of *see* have also explained why *see* favors co-occurrence with the meaning LESS CONTROL (roughly, what the tradition calls a direct object) more so than *look*. Previous analyses have all classified *look* as an intransitive verb, and have used this classification to explain why *look* co-occurs with prepositions (e.g., Levin 1993). But *look* does sometimes co-occur with the meaning LESS CONTROL, as for instance in *look me in the eye*. While some may posit this particular sequence to be a special construction (e.g., Wierzbicka 1988), no one has ever considered *looked him right across the table at the China Club* (Chapter 4, Example 51) a construction. Our analysis has shown that there is no need to posit a construction in either of these cases because the hypothesized meaning of *look*, together with the established hypothesis of the meanings of the Degree of Control System, can explain both why *look* disfavors co-occurrence with LESS CONTROL as well as why the two meanings are nonetheless sometimes chosen together.

While most of the predictions presented above were made on the basis of ATTENTION, some predictions followed from VISUAL as well. For example, we have seen that *look* co-occurs with visual attributes (e.g., *green*) at a higher than chance frequency in comparison to *seem* (which lacks VISUAL in its meaning). Or again, the hypothesis of VISUAL has explained why *look* co-occurs with forms denoting visual entities (e.g., *painting, tree*) at a higher than chance frequency in comparison to forms denoting abstract entities (e.g., *music, idea*).

One final note with respect to the quantitative predictions we have made. While previous CS analyses have tested their quantitative predictions on one or more texts each produced by a single person/author, this study has tested large-scale distributional predictions using COCA – a massive on-line corpus produced by thousands of speakers and writers. The use of COCA has allowed me to carry out many quantitative tests that would simply be impossible to do if done by "hand" using a couple or several books. Take, for instance, the predictions concerning the frequency of *but look* in comparison to *and look*, or of *looks to me* in comparison to *seems to me*; if done by hand, it would be practically impossible to gather enough tokens of either of those sequences to produce any significant results. This is true of virtually all the counts presented in this manuscript; none of them could have been done if all the tokens had to be found manually by reading through texts. The ability to search through the massive corpus on-line allows the analyst an unprecedented freedom, making it possible to test the frequency of virtually any sequence one wishes. While the quantitative predictions have been tested in this blind manner through large-scale searches, still, each and every prediction presented here has resulted from a qualitative analysis of an attested example that was found by hand. This methodological procedure underscores the fact that the proposed meaning hypotheses are intended to explain a speaker's choice of a particular sign on each occasion of its use. The confirmation of the predictions made in this manuscript have thus demonstrated that, through the use of a massive corpus, objective quantitative evidence can be brought to bear on the analysis proposed for a particular example, either supporting it or failing to support it.

# References

Blevins, J. (2012). Duality of patterning: absolute universal or statisticaltendency? *Language and Cognition* 4(4), 275–296. doi:10.1515/langcog-2012-0016

Bybee, J. (2002). Sequentiality as the basis of constituentstructure. In T. Givon & B. Malle (Eds.), *The evolution of language out of pre-language* (pp. 107–132). Amsterdam: John Benjamins. doi:10.1075/tsl.53.07byb

Bybee, J. (2006). From usage to grammar: The mind's response torepetition. *Language* 82(4), 711–733. doi:10.1353/lan.2006.0186

Bybee, J., & P. Hopper. (2001). Introduction to frequency and the emergence of linguisticstructure. In J. Bybee & P. Hopper (Eds.), *Frequency and the emergence of linguistic structure* (pp. 1–24). Amsterdam: John Benjamins. doi:10.1075/tsl.45.01byb

Clark, E. (1976). Universal categories: on the semantics of classifiers andchildren's early word meanings. In A. Juilland (Ed.), *Linguistic studies offered to Joseph Greenberg* (pp. 449–462). Saratoga, CA: Anma Libri.

Contini-Morava, E. (1995). Introduction. In E. Contini-Morava & B. Sussman Goldberg (Eds.), *Meaning as explanation: Advances in linguistic sign theory* (pp. 1–39). Berlin: Mouton de Gruyter.

Crupi, C. (2004). *But still a yet: the quest for a constant semantic value for Englishyet.* New Brunswick, NJ: State University of New Jersey dissertation.

Culler, J. (1976). *Ferdinand de Saussure.* Fonatan / Collins.

Davies, M. (2008–). *The corpus of contemporary American English: 450 million words, 1990–present.*

Davis, J. (2002). Rethinking the place of statistics in Columbia Schoolanalysis. In W. Reid, R. Otheguy & N. Stern (Eds.), *Signal, meaning, and message: perspectives on sign-basedlinguistics* (pp. 65–90). Amsterdam / Philadelphia: John Benjamins. doi:10.1075/sfsl.48.05dav

Davis, J. (2004). Revisiting the gap between meaning and message. In E. Contini-Morava, R. S. Kirsner & B. Rodriguez-Bachiller (Eds.), *Cognitive and communicative approaches to linguistic analysis* (pp. 155–174). Amsterdam / Philadelphia: John Benjamins. doi:10.1075/sfsl.51.08dav

Diver, W. (1969). The system of relevance of the Homeric verb. *Acta Linguistica Hafniensia 12*, 45–68. Revised and reprinted in A. Huffman & J. Davis. (Eds.), *Language: Communication and human behavior: The linguistic essays of William Diver* (pp. 135–159). Leiden / Boston: Brill.

Diver, W. (1974). Substance and value in linguistic analysis. *Semiotext(e) 1*, 11–30. Revised and reprinted A. Huffman & J. Davis. (Eds.), *Language: communication and human behavior: The linguistic essays of William Diver* (pp. 23–45). Leiden / Boston: Brill.

Diver, W. (1995). Theory. In E. Contini Morava & B. Sussman-Goldberg (Eds.), *Meaning as explanation: advances in linguistic sign theory* (pp. 43–114). Revised and reprinted A. Huffman & J. Davis. (Eds.), *Language: communication and human behavior: The linguistic essays of William Diver* (pp. 445–519). Leiden / Boston: Brill.

Diver, W. (2012). The elements of a science of a language. In A. Huffman & J. Davis (Eds.), *Language: communication and human behavior: The linguistic essays of William Diver* (pp. 65–84). Leiden / Boston: Brill.

Diver, W., J. Davis & W. Reid. (2012). Traditional grammar and its legacy in twentieth-centurylinguistics. In A. Huffman & J. Davis (Eds.), *Language: communication and human behavior: The linguistic essays of William Diver* (pp. 371–443). Leiden / Boston: Brill.

Goldberg, A. (1995). *Constructions – a construction grammar approach to argumentstructure.* Chicago and London: The University of Chicago Press.

Gruber, J. (1967). Look and see. *Language* 43(4), 937–947. doi:10.2307/411974

Haegeman, L. (1994). *Introduction to government and binding theory.* Second edition. Oxford UK and Cambridge USA: Blackwell.

Hatfield, G. (1998). Attention in early scientific psychology. In R. Wright (Ed.), *Visual attention* (pp. 3–25). New York / Oxford: Oxford University press.

Huffman, A. (1989). Teaching the English tenses. In W. Diver (Ed.), *Columbia University working papers in linguistics* (pp. 10.1–1065).

Huffman, A. (1997). *The categories of grammar: French lui andle.* Amsterdam: John Benjamins. doi:10.1075/slcs.30

Huffman, A. (2001). The Linguistics of William Diver and the Columbia School. *Word* 52, 29–68.

Huffman, A. (2006). Diver's Theory. In J. Davis, R. J. Gorup & N. Stern (Eds.), *Advances in functional linguistics: Columbia School beyond itsorigins* (pp. 41–62). Amsterdam / Philadelphia: John Benjamins. doi:10.1075/sfsl.57.05huf

Huffman, A. (2012). *Introduction: the enduring legacy of William Diver.* In A. Huffman & J. Davis (Eds.), *Language: communication and human behavior: The linguistic essays of William Diver* (pp. 9–20). Leiden / Boston: Brill.

Huffman, A. & J. Davis (Eds.). (2012). *Language: Communication and human behavior: The linguistic essays of William Diver.* Leiden / Boston: Brill.

Lakoff, G. (1993). The contemporary theory of metaphor. In A. Ortony (Ed.), Metaphor and thought, Volume 2 (pp. 202–251). Cambridge University Press.

Lakoff, G. and M. Johnson. (1980). *Metaphors we live by.* Chicago: University of Chicago Press.

Landau, B. and L. Gleitman. (1985). *Language and experience: evidence from the blind child.* Cambridge, MA: Harvard University Press.

Langacker, R. (2004). Form, meaning and behavior – the cognitive grammar analysisof double subject constructions. In E. Contini-Morava, R. S. Kirsner & B. Rodriguez-Bachiller (Eds.), *Cognitive and communicative approaches to linguistic analysis* (pp. 21–60). Amsterdam / Philadelphia: John Benjamins doi:10.1075/sfsl.51.03lan

Levin, B. (1993). *English verb classes and alternations: a preliminaryinvestigation.* Chicago and London: University of Chicago Press.

OED Online. (2015). "look, v."; "look, n." Oxford University Press. http://www.oed.com/view/Entry/110130?rskey=ltooak&result=2

Otheguy, R. (1995). When contact speakers talk, linguistic theorylistens. In E. Contini Morava & B. Sussman-Goldberg (Eds.), *Meaning as explanation: advances in linguistic sign theory* (pp. 213–242). Berlin / New York: Mouton de Gruyter. doi:10.1515/9783110907575.213

Otheguy, R. (2002). Saussurean anti-nomenclaturism in grammatical analysis: Acomparative theoretical perspective. In W. Reid, R. Otheguy & N. Stern (Eds.), *Signal, meaning, and message: perspectives on sign-basedlinguistics* (pp. 373–403). Amsterdam / Philadelphia: John Benjamins doi:10.1075/sfsl.48.18oth

Otheguy, R., B. Rodriguez-Bachiller & E. Canals. (2004). Length of the extra-information phrase as a predictor of wordorder. In E. Contini-Morava, R. S. Kirsner & B. Rodriguez-Bachiller (Eds.), *Cognitive and communicative approaches to linguistic analysis* (pp. 325–340). Amsterdam / Philadelphia: John Benjamins  doi:10.1075/sfsl.51.18oth

Pierce, J. (1985). The nature of English grammar. English teaching forum, July: 2–8.

Reid, W. (1974). The Saussurean sign as a control in linguisticanalysis. *Semiotext(e)*1.31–53.

Reid, W. (1991). *Verb and noun number in English: a functional explanation.* London: Langman.

Reid, W. (1995). Quantitative Analysis in Columbia School Theory. In E. Contini Morava & B. Sussman-Goldberg (Eds.), *Meaning as explanation: advances in linguistic sign theory* (pp. 115–152). Berlin / New York: Mouton de Gruyter.  doi:10.1515/9783110907575.115

Reid, W. (2004). Monosemy, Homonymy and Polysemy. In E. Contini-Morava, R. S. Kirsner & B. Rodriguez-Bachiller (Eds.), *Cognitive and communicative approaches to linguistic analysis* (pp. 93–130). Amsterdam / Philadelphia: John Benjamins.  doi:10.1075/sfsl.51.06rei

Reid, W. (2011). The communicative function of English verb number. *Natural language linguistic theory*, 29, 1087–1146.  doi:10.1007/s11049-011-9154-0

Saussure, F. (1916). *Cours de linguistique generale.* Translated by Roy Harris as Course in general linguistics. La Salle, Illinois: Open Court Classics, 1972 [1986].

Swan, M. (1980). *Practical English usage.* Oxford University Press.

Sweetser, E. (1990). *From etymology to pragmatics: metaphorical and cultural aspects ofsemantic structure.* Cambridge University Press.  doi:10.1017/CBO9780511620904

Tobin, Y. (1993). *Aspect in the English verb: process and result in language.* London and New York: Longman.

Tomasello, M. (2003). *Constructing a language – a usage-based theory of language acquisition.* Cambridge, Massachusetts and London, England: Harvard University Press.

Vendler, Z. (1957). Verbs and Times. *Philosophical Review* 56, 143–160.  doi:10.2307/2182371

Wierzbicka, A. (1988). *The Semantics of Grammar.* Amsterdam / Philadelphia: John Benjamins.  doi:10.1075/slcs.18

Wolff, C. (1738). *Psychologia empirica.* Frankfurt and Leipzig: Officina Libraria Rengeriana. Cited by section number.

# Index